COACHING LIFE

by
Dr Tony Fusco

© Copyright 2022 Dr Tony Fusco
Print Edition

All Rights Reserved. No part of this publication may be reproduced, distributed or transmitted in any form or by any means, or stored in a database or retrieval system, without the prior written permission of the publisher.

ISBN 978-1-3999-3298-1

Published by Three-Dimensional Press

Cover Design by 100Covers.com

To T M W

Contents

Introduction	vii
Chapter One: Coaching, Life and Latte	1
Chapter Two: Coaching, Life and the Lakes	40
Chapter Three: Coaching, Life and Lockdown	84
Chapter Four: Coaching, Life and Leadership	125

COACHING LIFE
INTRODUCTION

THE SEEDS OF 'Coaching Life' were planted in southwest Turkey over a decade ago when my partner and I stayed at a hotel on the Turkish coast of Mugla. It was our first trip to the area and in between dips in the sea, both myself and my partner, who fortunately is also a coach, immersed ourselves in Irvin Yalom's bestseller, *Love's Executioner*. An enthralling read and one that gave us much to discuss after running the gauntlet of the evening buffet-bar.

For readers unfamiliar with Irvin Yalom, two facts are immediately pertinent. Fact one: Yalom is a master existential psychotherapist, and this means his books are an important read. Fact two: Yalom is also a master storyteller, and this makes his books a joy to read.

Over several years and several more trips to Turkey our accommodation tastes grew ever more rural and remote. And so it was, on one particular trip we found ourselves in a remote rustic idyll. This was nice, but the thing with rural hillside idylls is that they're miles from anywhere.

The days flew by, but evening always presented us with a choice. Smarten up and drive to town or kick back and boil some pasta. It was no real contest. We spent each evening on the veranda putting the world to rights and consuming unhealthy amounts of pasta, minty cigarettes and sharp local wine.

During one evening discussion about life and living, we hit upon an idea. Why not write a version of *Love's Executioner* for the coaching world? Instead of tales of therapy we could write about people's coaching journeys. Why not, we thought? And so, the drunken seeds were sown.

In the years between, I completed my doctoral studies, in which I researched *authentic leadership development*. This too was influenced by Yalom's work as a group therapist as I devised a group-coaching approach to ALD. Further inspired by his existential approach, I developed an approach that forced leaders to look square on at the existential matters of their lives and careers, such as their values, their purpose, their life stories and self-identities. Heavy stuff for leadership development, but in most cases, utterly transformational. By the end of it all, I was done with academic writing and thoughts returned to my own humble version of *Love's Executioner*.

It was after his two seminal textbooks on group and existential psychotherapy that Yalom turned his inestimable talents to fiction and what he called his 'teaching novels'. Along with *Love's Executioner* heavyweight titles such as *The Schopenhauer Cure* and *When Nietzsche Wept* belie featherweight reads based around character encounters as enthralling as you are likely to find in any fictional genre.

Only when you put these books down does their magic become apparent. Having been thoroughly engrossed in their tales, you gradually become aware of all you've learnt. Not just about the therapeutic encounter, but about life and living and what it means to be human. Yalom encases his teaching in such stylish and enigmatic writing you have no idea of the learning that is quietly taking place off stage.

This brings us to my own small attempt at what I term 'educational fiction'. A brazen attempt to emulate Irv's own genre perhaps, but there the similarities end. Why? First, my own efforts are of course microscopic in comparison to a Stanford-trained psychiatric genius. Also, I have taken a slightly different route in the storytelling. Rather than study individual encounters, with the omniscient commentary of the therapist/coach, I have decided to invite the reader on a different kind of journey.

In *Coaching Life* we follow the adventures of two workmates, Jasper Oran and Simone Marshall through the different stages of their coaching journey. We follow them as they progress from being coaching clients and coach trainees, to coach practitioners themselves, first inside their organisation and then outside. Along the way we eavesdrop on their conversations as they discuss their coaching experiences; how they react, what they learn and how all this impacts their outlook on their careers and their lives.

Chapter One of *Coaching Life* joins Jasper and Simone in a London coffee shop as they commence their own coaching with the help of three coaches: a Cognitive coach, a Gestalt coach and an Existential coach. Chapter Two accompanies them to the Lake District where they undertake some initial coach training of their own. Chapter Three watches as they start to practice during the pandemic and the unique challenges that presents. Chapter Four then joins them on a leadership group-coaching retreat. And beyond that, who knows. We will have to see what paths they choose.

Their story isn't designed to either directly teach

coaching or explain exactly what happens in coaching. There are shelves full of quite excellent textbooks and how-to guides. What I have tried to do in this book is offer an insight into how it *feels* to coach and be coached. The sorts of experiences people get from different types of coaching, how they might react, what they might learn how it can change them.

My aim is therefore no more ambitious than to offer the interested reader a light fictional read around the topic coaching. Whether you're interested in practicing coaching or having coaching, the tale of Simone and Jasper, their highs and lows, revelations and reckonings will hopefully give you some useful insight into this fascinating subject.

Serefe!

Dr Tony Fusco
Malvern, UK. 2022

Chapter One
COACHING, LIFE AND LATTE

JASPER IS STANDING with Simone in the kitchenette making morning coffee when Liam corners them.

"So, here's the situation. HR has been approached by a local university who want to undertake some research into workplace coaching. The boss is keen and asked me to find some recruits."

Jasper looks up from his mug, puzzled. Simone does the same.

"You've both mentioned coaching before so I thought you might be interested. Apparently, there's three sessions on offer with three different types of coaches. Hang on a minute." Liam flicks through some loose pages inside his notebook. "There's a Cognitive coach – Mitch Aaron, a Gestalt coach – Lorna Martine and an Existential coach – Yared Sorensen. And before you ask, I've absolutely no idea what any of these things are."

Simone and Jasper look questioningly at each other.

"If you're up for it, great, if not I'll find someone else, it's no bother. I just need it off my to-do list."

"It's only a few hours of our life, I guess," Simone says, "and I am a bit curious."

Jasper shrugs. "Sure, why not?"

Liam hands them both a sheet of paper with the summary information and contact details. "OK, book the sessions and let me know how you get on. Sound good?"

Simone and Jasper nod.

"Great." The divisional director walks back towards the door then stops and turns. "Now, I know the coaching is confidential, but when you're done, if you can report back in broad terms about how you got on, the impact it's had, what you've changed etcetera, then I can relay that back upstairs." He stands in the doorway with raised questioning eyebrows. "Agreed?"

"Agreed," Jasper and Simone reply in unison.

"Good luck," Liam calls over his shoulder as he leaves.

"Well, I wasn't expecting that." Jasper blows out the breath he'd been holding.

"Me neither."

"Any idea what any of these things are?" Jasper asks, studying his sheet of paper.

"Not a clue," Simone says.

"Should be interesting, shouldn't it, talking about ourselves solid for a few hours. When did you last do that?"

"I don't think I ever have," Simone replies.

"Me neither. How about we meet up when we're having the sessions? We can share the gory details. Well, maybe not everything, of course. What do you say?"

Simone thinks for a moment. "OK."

"We can meet at the little coffee shop we went to after that client meeting last year."

"The one up the alley?" Simone asks, stirring her coffee.

"That's the one."

As they head back to their desks, Jasper thinks

how random life is. He and Simone have worked in the same office, at opposite ends of the same floor, since the office relocation five years ago, but they've never been more than passing acquaintances attending the occasional meeting together. Even though they joined the firm at the same time and are both in their late thirties, they've never really socialised after work, their interactions limited to discussing office politics whenever they share a coffee.

He sits down at his desk and looks out into the gloom, over the rooftops in the rough direction of the alley and the coffee shop. *This is going to be interesting.*

THE COFFEE SHOP heaves with damp bodies jostling for position to order and collect. The background noise is loud and shrill, and the baristas do their utmost to make coffee-making look and sound like a full-contact sport. They push past each other behind their small counter, shouting orders among themselves, crashing crockery into the sink, and emptying the metal scoops with regular violent clangs; all the while the coffee machine hisses and spits.

Jasper winces as he enters. *This is not the quiet cosy enclave I remember. I'm not in the mood for this place.*

"Hell's teeth, Simone – why did we choose here again?"

Simone looks up. "And a good morning to you too."

"Sorry." Jasper sits down on a small wooden chair. He shakes the rain from his coat, folds it over a stool and leans forward to try again. "Dear Simone, my new and trusted coaching-buddy, who has even got the milky coffees in, how the devil are you?"

"Thank you. I'm fine, Jasper. But you don't seem overly happy, if you don't mind me saying." She pushes Jasper's latte towards him.

I'm flippin not. He thinks as he reaches for his coffee.

"How was it?" Simone asks.

"Intense." Jasper nudges aside a small damp pile of raincoats and umbrellas with his foot and puts down his briefcase.

"Really?"

"Oh yeah. Mornings are grim enough back at the office anyway, but this week I have the extra special treat of being bashed over the head for two hours straight. Nice."

Simone apologises as two sarcastically smiling city types retrieve their umbrellas and coats.

Jasper notices that he and Simone are also wearing the same city uniform of grey suit and white shirt. *She looks like she's just walked here straight from a fashion show and check the state of me. I look like a crumpled bag-of-crap.*

"You're looking very dapper," he says, waving his hand towards her black cashmere coat and glossy red gloves.

"Thank you, and you were very brave doing that first session." Simone smiles sympathetically. "What was on the agenda?"

Jasper brushes non-existent crumbs off the table with the flat of his palm. "Well," he starts, "the Cognitive coach informed me that my thinking is crooked, distorted, illogical and irrational. How's that for a start? Whoever thinks coaching is just a nice cosy chat is way off." He taps his wooden stirrer against his mug. "Apparently, I'm not the rational person I thought I was. Seems I have major kinks in my not-so-super-logical brain. Nice start, eh?" He empties a sugar sachet into his mug and then leans back. "Thing is, though..." He folds his arms, bites his bottom lip and gazes outside into the dim and soaked alleyway.

"Thing is?" Simone lightly taps the table with her spoon.

"When he pointed them out to me, I recognised immediately every single one of the errors he was talking about. And that Mitch dude was not how I imagined a coach to be. Aren't they supposed to be like counsellors? Make us feel better, happier? Help with our understanding of ourselves and stuff like that?" He looks to Simone, hoping to find her equally aghast.

She blows into her latte and without making eye contact asks, "Isn't he doing that? If he's showing you ways you're not thinking clearly or straight, isn't he helping you?"

Didn't feel that way. Jasper thinks as he repeatedly slaps another sugar sachet against the edge of the table. "I guess. I'm just a bit bewildered at the minute to be honest. Also, a bit irked that a complete stranger can know so much about me and how I go about my thinking." He looks plaintively at Simone. "Are we really that predictable?"

Simone smiles, rescues the sugar sachet from his grasp and returns it to the bowl. "And this is just session one," she says. "There's going to be much more of this, you know. Are you sure you're going to be up for it after this first experience?"

"I guess." Jasper throws his wooden stirrer into his half-empty mug. *I'm not giving up that easily.*

"Anyway, my turn." Simone pulls on her overcoat and unzips her sky blue umbrella. "I've got my first session with Yared, the Existential coach. Wish me luck."

Jasper watches her head for the door. *What the hell have we let ourselves in for?*

SIMONE RETURNS TO a much quieter scene and sees Jasper on his laptop, nodding along to whatever is coming through his huge headphones. *Oblivious*, she thinks.

He sees her, pulls off his headphones and pushes out a chair. "Two ticks, I'll get the brews in."

When he returns, Simone is sitting motionless, her unfocussed gaze somewhere out the window.

"So?" Jasper asks as he sits back down.

"Interesting," Simone replies.

"It must have been. You look like you've left half yourself back there. You OK?"

"I think so." Simone's stare remains fixed. *I think so.*

"So, what was on the existentialist's agenda?" Jasper slides over a large mug of latte.

Simone blinks and shakes her head. "Everything, nothing, all sorts." She reaches for the coffee.

"Excellent, well, that's clear," Jasper says, sarcastically. "Not sure what Liam's going to do with that in his report."

Simone stares down into her coffee. "We didn't talk about anything specifically job-related, at first anyway, more about the meaning of things. Like my role, my career, even my life. We literally sat there discussing the meaning of life, which seems slightly bizarre. I don't recall having that sort of conversation with anyone before, ever, not previous boyfriends or girlfriends or anyone." She slowly raises her mug. "The session seemed to have a real philosophical slant to it, and I'm sure he quoted Marcus Aurelius to me at one point."

"How do you know that?" Jasper asks.

"Know what?"

"That he quoted Marcus Aurelius."

"I think I recognised it," she says.

Jasper looks intently at Simone while chewing his wooden stirrer. "From where?"

"My degree."

"Oh yeah. What degree did you do?"

"Classics," she replies, to which Jasper beams a broad grin, clenching his stirrer between his teeth. "Well, you kept that quiet. Who'd have thought it? I had you down as a definite MBAer for sure. No offence."

"Thanks – none taken."

"Well, come on. You've definitely got a whiff of the Arthur Andersen about you, haven't you? Crisp white consultant's shirt and shiny black consultant's folder. You look like LSE's finest."

"Yes, I know, thank you." Simone self-consciously adjusts her expensive suit jacket.

Jasper narrows his eyes. "So?"

"So what?"

"Come on, Miss Andersen. So, did all this meaning-of-life stuff do any good?"

Simone sits upright with her hands folded in her lap. *Did it do any good?* "Not sure yet, but it's left me feeling curiously vulnerable somehow. Like someone just asked me to confront my own existence, square on. Which is exactly what he did, I guess, but I'm not entirely sure I signed up for that. I thought the coaching would help me work on issues with my team, colleagues, clients, that sort of thing, not ask me to talk about the meaning of life."

Jasper listens intently.

"Anyway, it certainly made me question a lot of stuff I never have before."

"Like?"

"Like my values. Not in an esoteric, fluffy way, but in a concrete practical way. What my personal operating principles are if you like. Which is a tricky one to fully grasp at the best of times yourself, let alone try and articulate to someone else. He asked me where my values come from, in my personal history. Not just what they are but where they come from. All of which led to an interesting deep dive into my back story as you can imagine."

Jasper nods, rapt.

"I also had to explore how these values appear in my day-to-day management and leadership. He asked me what it's like when I'm able to live my values at work and what it's like when I'm not. I didn't realise so much of what we do in management and leadership is inherently value laden. Almost everything we do, implicitly or explicitly, is based on some underlying belief or assumption. I've never thought about it in that way before. You just crack on, don't you?" Simone nods to herself.

"So, what are those values?" asks Jasper.

Simone looks straight through him. "That's the big question, isn't it?" she says with an unfocussed gaze. "I'm not entirely sure yet." *But the lid is now well and truly ripped off that little Pandora's box.*

BACK AT THEIR coffee spot the following Tuesday, Jasper presents two blueberry muffins.

"Energy for the sessions ahead," he says. Then

through a mouthful of muffin suddenly announces, "My mum named me after one of those existentialists, you know."

"Really?"

"Yeah." He brushes crumbs off his shirt. "Mum was into philosophy big time when I was born. She had a whole room filled with shelves of books, and I remember her waving one at me once when I was a kid, telling me I was named after its author. Now, who was it?" Jasper closes his eyes and taps both temples with sticky forefingers.

Simone neatly folds a napkin and dabs the corners of her mouth.

"Jasper-Jasper-Jasper Conran. No, Karl. Karl Jaspers. That's it, Karl Jaspers. He was an Existential psychiatrist, I learnt years later when I was bothered enough to look at the book. What on earth does one of those do?"

He studies Simone. "You could've come the same route actually, couldn't you?"

"How do you mean?"

"Well, you know Jean-Paul Sartre, right?" Jasper says.

"From the office?"

"Hilarious. No, from the Paris Left Bank circa World War Two."

"Teeny bit before my time I'm glad to say, but I have a vague awareness of him."

"Well, he was a big deal writer, wasn't he, and his big deal writer girlfriend was called Simone de Beauvoir. Do you think your parents called you after her?"

Simone laughs and shakes her head as if taken aback by the sheer implausibility of the idea. "Very unlikely, I'd say. Dad was an architect and Mum was a maths teacher, both Ealing born and bred. The nearest they ever got to Paris was probably Brighton."

She doesn't seem completely satisfied with that. I wonder if...

"How about your parents?" Simone asks straight back.

Jasper again throws his wooden stirrer into the empty coffee mug, now like a form of punctuation. He slides back in his chair, shoves his hands deep in his pockets and drops his chin on his chest. He hesitates – *well, here goes nothing.* "Mum was a sweetheart, loved her philosophy and poetry and was a real hippy at heart, which makes it even more bizarre how she hooked up with my father who, frankly, was a cartoon character."

Simone waits, expectantly.

"Truth is, he had another family."

Simone's eyes widen.

"I kid you not, he literally had another family. I've only ever seen that stuff in movies, but the guy actually raised another family – somewhere up north."

"Nooo." Simone exhales.

Yep. Jasper remains reclined, staring at his feet. "He was an engineer and used to tell us he was working offshore on the rigs, four weeks on, four weeks off, while all the time he was raising two families on a monthly rota. Turns out he worked in a power station in the Midlands, so he just commuted up and down the motorway between them up north and us down south. Can you believe that?" Jasper leans forward, drumming the tabletop with his fingertips.

Simone leans forward and places her hands on top of his to still his drumming. "Jesus, Jasper. What does that even do to a person growing up?"

"Makes you want to have a family of your own and make it the best ever, is one thing I guess. But it also makes you want to never have one. I envy my friends with their nice, secure family units sometimes, but weirdly, I also feel a bit superior to them."

Simone looks perplexed.

"It feels like my life has a Shakespearean vibe about it, one that perhaps gives me a greater perspective than other mere mortals. There may indeed be more in my heaven and earth than others can fathom in their philosophy."

"Seriously, now Hamlet quotes?"

"Absolutely, and fitting too, I'd say. Is this whole coaching thing not Hamlet-esque? To thine own self be true … and all that."

"True," Simone says.

"It made me realise that if you can choose to have two families and make that your reality, then pretty much anything is fair game. So, it was life on my own terms from there on. I'd survived that tragic part of my life so I could take that experience out into the world as my own secret weapon. What was the worst that could possibly happen after that?" Jasper exhales. *I didn't expect to blurt that little lot out so quick.*

Jasper looks around the coffee shop. *I wonder how many of these yummy mummies and gobby yuppies have been through that kind of crap?* He sees a couple at the opposite window, who both look like they've been crying. *What's their story? I wonder. I guess we all have our own secret crosses to bear.* He looks back at Simone. *I wonder what hers is.* He shakes himself out of his reverie. "Anyway, how about you, any dramas growing up?"

"Oh Lord, yes. My life was a real Shakespearean tragicomedy," Simone says sarcastically. "Unfortunately, both the tragedy and the comedy were how painfully dull it was. Between birth and Uni, nothing much happened at all, just a dull, dull life. I had no problems at school or home and no problems with friends or boyfriends – mainly because I didn't have many of either, to be fair." She grasps her knees. "A dull girl living a dull life – that's it."

Jasper stares at her, unconvinced. "Uh-huh."

"OK," Simone concedes. "The shirt wasn't always this crisp and white. I did the usual things at Uni. I had the odd drink and dalliance. But not nearly as much as everyone else seemed to. My dullness probably followed me up there from Middlesex."

"To where?"

"Durham. Should've been the time of my life, but the most this dull Ealing girl got from it was a decent degree from a good uni. Double first – woo hoo! Just enough to get me into a dull graduate programme in a dull firm. And fast-forward fifteen years, here I am, talking about my dull life with you, not massively life-affirming if I'm honest. No offence."

"None taken. Frankly, coming from the other end of the tragic-family spectrum, dull doesn't sound so bad to me."

"Yes, I know, and I feel bad moaning about it. I just always craved at least a little bit of adventure beyond the nine to five, you know?"

I most certainly do, sister. "What about siblings?"

Simone shrugs. "Even that's bland. One perfect older brother, loving son who's great at his studies and his sport and doted on by both my parents and me – yuck! Seriously, just a little drama would have been nice. Nice, argh... even my idea of drama is vanilla."

"Perhaps one of your parents led a double life too?" Jasper says.

"You're kidding, they went nowhere. Mum went to school, Dad went to the office, and then they both came home again. I subscribe to the mix of nature and nurture, and fear I've inherited both their genes and their outlook. Here I am, with a privileged path up the corporate ladder, and I'm starting to think that maybe I don't want it. Maybe it's just another kind of dullness that I'm pursuing blindly."

Simone flumps back and folds her arms. "I think I've just been on autopilot ever since joining the company. Taking all the development opportunities they put my way, this coaching included. Taking the promotions, they somehow think I deserve and presume I want. I don't even stop to consider whether I do or not. I just keep going. Me and my crisp white shirt and shiny black folder." She darts Jasper a narrow-eyed look. "Thanks for that."

Jasper is none too happy with his lot at the firm either. Background reading around existential coaching has helped him understand why a sense of meaning and purpose are so important to him and has given name to his increasing disquiet at work. The operational efficiencies the company pay him to achieve have all but lost any sense of meaning for him.

"I'm not that happy at the moment either, if I'm honest," he says.

"Why not?"

"I'm just in the wrong place and have been for too long."

"How so?" Simone asks.

"If our firm's a ship, then they've definitely got me holed up in the engine room. The mechanics of the operation are banging and booming around my head, all day long, KPIs this and SLAs that – it drives me nuts. I know the metrics are important, they power the engine of the ship, but I simply don't belong in the engine room. I belong up top. Not because that's where the top brass is, but because that's where the views are. That's where you steer and navigate."

"I was never great with metaphors, to be honest," Simone says.

"Look around. See all these baristas at the counter doing their stuff? Well, they're here working the engine room – hell, it even looks like one behind there with all the chrome pipes and the clattering and banging."

Simone cranes her neck to look over.

"If I was working for this company, this is not where I would want to be. I'd want to be up at head office working on their long-term strategic stuff. Exploring potential new markets or mergers. Examining new demographics, new products, new tech. Scanning the horizon and deciding on where to steer the ship next, do you know what I mean?"

"I think so," Simone says.

"It's how my brain is wired; I love mapping connections and patterns. Working out the flow of cause and effect within systems – organisational, mechanical, whatever." Jasper looks intently at Simone. "But down in the engine room where they have me, it's all about monitoring the flaming metrics. Smoothing rough edges to increase efficiencies and cost savings, one miserable little increment at a time. I tell you, Simone, it's killing me. I need out. I need some light and air."

They both stare at the table in silence until Jasper eventually laughs.

"Ha! You know what's just dawned on me? I don't think Liam has a clue where this whole coaching thing could lead, does he? Not a clue."

JASPER IS FIRST in the coffee shop for their next rendezvous. "Sooooo, how was your Gestalt coaching then?" he asks as Simone approaches their table.

"Different," she says.

"How so?" Jasper puts down his phone as Simone drops her folder and coat straight onto the floor and flops into the chair. She stretches for her coffee, already lined-up.

"Bizarrely, she got me up doing experiments to help me understand what I was feeling in my body in response to various things."

"Go on."

"I was talking about how I feel uncomfortable in a lot of what my job entails – meetings about this and meetings about that, all day, every day. I feel way out of my comfort zone in most of them. It's not that I feel intellectually inadequate, but more and more, I seem to be involved in strategy meetings, your captain's deck stuff, and I hate it."

Jasper gives her a wistful smile.

Don't get me wrong. I'm really pleased they're getting me involved from a career perspective, but, my God, it's tedious." Simone looks cross-eyed at Jasper to make her point.

He taps his spoon on her knuckles. "Experiment?"

"Right. She got me to sit at a large meeting table and told me to imagine I was sitting in one of these tedious meetings and asked me to say how I was feeling. Not just emotionally, but physically too. It was a revelation. It turns out I'm in these meetings with tension in my stomach, my hands, my chest, the lot, a real stress ball. But how can that be? How can I be stressed and bored at the same time?" She looks expectantly at Jasper. "Seriously, that's not a rhetorical question. How can you be tense and bored simultaneously?"

"Dunno, what did the coach say?"

"That's the other part of it, she said very little. She just shared what she was experiencing, of what I was experiencing, if that makes any sense."

"Not really." Jasper gives a cross-eyed look of his own.

"No, I can't make sense of it myself yet. I think that needs to percolate for a while." Simone closes her eyes. *Stressed and bored? I get the bored bit, but I really didn't know they were making me so stressed. About what though?*

"Anyway, how was existentialism for you?" She opens her eyes and settles into her chair.

"Right up my street as it happens. I remember as an older kid I'd browse mum's bookshelves and I quite liked some of the philosophy stuff. I couldn't entirely get my head round it at that age, but I still felt it speaking to me on some level. If I ever did a degree, I think I'd quite fancy my chances at that. Big fat philosophical ideas and systems of thought, all good non-practical stuff."

Jasper gazes through the window, watching the lunchtime parade pass by. The sun is shining today, and the noise of the coffee house just an agreeable burble.

"You've not got a degree?" Simone asks.

"Nope. I was a bit of a basket case at school really. My folks wrote me off, teachers wrote me off. I nearly wrote myself off too."

"You're in a decent job now though, aren't you? So, what turned it around?"

"I think it was that whole deal with my Dad, so

I've got him to thank for that at least." Jasper tuts. "Anyway, I know you've got to process today's session, but did you discover anything else other than you're a stressy-Simone when you're in these big hotshot meetings of yours?"

"I think I did, actually." Simone puts down her mug, leans forward and, in a conspiratorial tone, whispers, "I think I'm in the wrong job."

Jasper leans forward and in his own hushed tone replies, "Shit!"

Simone nods and stares straight at him. *Shit indeed.*

"You know what the great Homer would say to that?" Jasper asks quietly.

"Do tell," she whispers back.

"Doh!" he shouts and throws himself backwards.

Idiot. Simone sits upright, shaking her head. "I thought you were going to offer me some timeless wisdom from Homer's *Iliad* or *Odyssey*. But I get Homer flipping Simpson."

Jasper looks at her straight-faced. "But seriously, it is a pretty big doh, though, isn't it? So, where's that come from?"

"I realised even when I was sitting at that big table that I don't really belong there. I don't get what they're saying half the time, and I'm not interested in what they're saying the rest of the time. I feel like an imposter, but not an imposter who wants to front it out and play the game, more an imposter who just wants to be somewhere else. Somewhere I don't feel like a stressed-out imposter." She leans back.

"Well, y'know, Simone, without wanting to sound all guru-like, they say it's not what your imposter says to you – 'cos let's face it we've all got one – it's what we say back to it that really matters. So, where are you telling yours you'd rather be?"

"With my team working on our own stuff," she says. "The coach asked me when and where I feel in flow, when I feel balanced and focussed and the opposite of bored and stressed. Turns out that's with my team. It seems stressy-Simone, as you call her, is all about her team."

"I can see that, actually," Jasper says. "Whenever I walk through your department there always seems to be a positive buzz about the place, which is palpably different from most of the others I visit."

When Simone realises Jasper isn't kidding, she is momentarily stunned. *Wow. The first bit of positive feedback I've ever received as a manager, and it comes by accident in some random coffee shop.* "I don't care about the relentless grind of quarterly figures or the next tranche of company updates or revamped strategic objectives and financial blah blahs. Even though it's my job. And I certainly don't care about all the petty bickering or the pointless politics." She rolls her eyes. "What really satisfies me is managing my team and everything that that involves – the good, the bad and the ugly." She sounds energised even just talking about it.

Jasper nods as another sharped dressed city type asks to borrow an unused chair.

"The good is great, of course, but even the bad and the ugly are OK too, because I see a purpose to them. I can see the difference it makes to my team. The good is when we're cohesive and flying as a unit. The bad is the poor performance stuff. And the ugly is the odd disciplinary and tribunal, because the firm can be harsh when it wants to be, can't it? But it's all good, because it's all about the people and how they perform and not about stock price or branding or market share or whatever other blah blahs."

"Wow," Jasper says. "And you got all that from sitting at the large table feeling how tense you were, and the coach sharing their experience of your experience and what not?"

"Kind of, yes. She asked me to pace the room and imagine I was in a more constructive, positive environment, and when I chose my department, I physically changed. Seriously, physically changed. Gone were all my tense bits, and I just felt a lightness and I even began smiling. I pictured my team right there and just wanted to get back to them." Simone smiles and shakes her head.

"And how are you feeling now?"

"A little conflicted, to be honest. It's kind of assumed that me and my crisp shirt and shiny folder are heading up the ladder. But I know that'll mean I leave behind team management and enter the increasingly surreal and abstract world of pie-chart presentations and Gordon Gekko wannabes." Simone sits quietly for a few moments. *What to do with this little bombshell?* Then suddenly she shifts to face Jasper square on. "So?"

"So, what?" replies Jasper, slowly and suspiciously.

"So, what do I do?"

"Oh no. No, no, no, no, no. If we've learnt anything from this coaching, it is *not* to give advice or tell people what to do. Am I right?"

"You are, but you're not my coach."

"And thank Christ for that. I'm also not your mother, your brother, your boyfriend or your father. Go ask them for career advice."

Simone puts on a sulky look and flicks coffee froth at Jasper. "You're no help at all, are you."

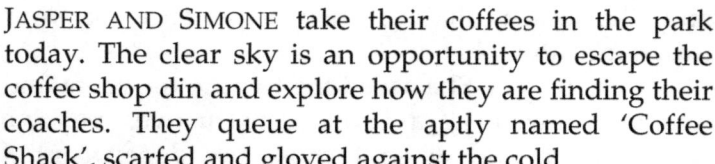

JASPER AND SIMONE take their coffees in the park today. The clear sky is an opportunity to escape the coffee shop din and explore how they are finding their coaches. They queue at the aptly named 'Coffee Shack', scarfed and gloved against the cold.

"So, how did you find working with the Gestalt coach?" Jasper stomps the ground to magic up some warmth while they stand in line.

Simone folds up her cashmere collar and gazes around the park, contemplating the question earnestly as she always does. "Lorna was still and serene," she eventually says.

"Yeah?"

"Yeah, I could've sat with her all day. She had such a calming presence."

They grab their coffees and wander to a bench.

"In no time at all I was talking about things I've simply never shared with anyone, and she just smiled sweetly, but oh-so knowingly."

Jasper prises the lid off his latte. "I wonder how much these folks get paid for listening and smiling sweetly."

"That's not really what it's about though, is it? It's her ability to make me feel I can talk to her about anything and then help me identify and explore various themes and patterns in what I do say. That's what they train for and are paid for."

"True. So, what *did* you talk about?"

"Lots, even family stuff in the end. Not sure where that came from, but it was clearly present for me. Stuff I've kept to myself all my life, and there I was, sharing the lot with saintly Lorna within the first session.

Jasper takes off his black gloves with his teeth and

muffles through a mouth full of wool, "Family stuff?"

"I told her some of the feelings I have towards my parents that I'm really not proud of, that somehow felt relevant in the moment."

"And?" Jasper stuffs his gloves into his Crombie pockets.

"She just smiled, radiating warmth, compassion and understanding. Not a trace of judgement. I mean, not a shred. And believe me, I was looking for it, intently. She just emanated a worldly essence of 'You'll have to go a long way to shock me, my dear. I've heard it all before. All of it.'" Simone cups her coffee for warmth, oddly at ease for someone who's been baring her soul to a stranger. "So, I dumped on her. My maddest, baddest bits that I've never shared with anyone. I felt a searing moment of opportunity, so she got the lot, both barrels."

They look at each other and burst out laughing.

"And do you know what she said to me?" Simone asks, composing herself.

"Nope."

"After hearing my innermost crappiness?"

"Go on."

"Welcome to the human race." Simone blows on her coffee and shakes her head. "Welcome to the human race. I could have wept."

They sit in silence for a while, clutching their coffees. Eventually, Simone looks over at her companion. She wrinkles her forehead, purses her lips, and gives Jasper her penetrating stare, the particular stare that says, 'This bit is serious.' "You just don't get that in normal life, do you?"

"Get what?"

"That kind of acceptance."

"What kind?" Jasper asks.

"The unconditional kind."

Jasper silently pulls his mouth down into a gurn. *Hell no, but what do you expect? We're all shits.*

"Who do you have, Jasper? Friend, family, colleague, girlfriend, ex-girlfriend, who? Who knows you one hundred per cent, everything?"

Jasper feels queasy at Simone's question, but she doesn't relent.

"All of your innards, Jasper," she says, jabbing his stomach through his overcoat. "Your hopes, dreams, fears, anxieties, insecurities. Your weirdness and your wickedness. Who knows all that, Jasper? Who knows all that and accepts you anyway?"

Feeling slightly blindsided and bemused, Jasper offers typical humorous deflection, "Well, no one yet, but by the sound of it, that Lorna might be my go-to girl."

Simone isn't letting up.

"She may well be, but that's the thing. We can't normally share this side of ourselves with those around us, can we? Can we?" Her stare persists, keeping Jasper on his mark.

"I guess not," he replies. "Why is that do you think?"

"Because all our relationships are riddled with tariffs. That's my theory anyway."

"What do you mean, tariffs?"

"Everything's conditional, isn't it?" Simone states, more than asks. "All our relationships have terms and conditions. Implicit expectations, with sanctions and penalties for all deviations and transgressions."

Jasper gurns again and blows into his cupped hands. "How do you mean, terms and conditions?"

"Like, you do that for me and be there for me in that way, and I'll do this for you and be here for you in this way. If you and I were married, Jasper, heaven help us, we may never openly speak of tariffs in all our married years together, but they would always be there. Glued to the underneath of the *Welcome* mat at the front door or stitched behind that stupid *Home Sweet Home* sign hanging in the hallway. They'll drip over our precious picture frames in the lounge and our ridiculous his-and-hers cushions in the bedroom."

Jaspers gurn turns into a broad smile. He gets exactly what Simone is saying, and if ever there was going to be a moment that cements their friendship, this is it. *I may never have to endure the trial of choosing soft furnishings with you, Simone Marshall, but I reckon I've found the perfect travelling partner for this journey.* Despite a slightly buttoned-up persona, he is finding that she is bold of mind and adventurous of spirit. What more could he ask? "See, you're not so bad with metaphors, are you?" He quips, keeping his deeper musings to himself.

Simone pierces him again with the stare. "One," she demands, keeping her eyes on him but sinking her chin into her scarf.

"One what?"

"Give me one example from your life where that is not the case. Who have you got?"

Jasper takes a moment, like he's chewing something horribly wholesome. Something that may be good for the system but still tastes grim. He watches a pair of squirrels chase each other through the dead leaves as his brain scans a record of every significant relationship he can remember having.

Simone sees him scanning and waits for the results.

Finally, the results are in, and Jasper is ready to announce his findings. "Yeah, fair enough. No one."

Simone appears satisfied. "Come on, let's check out the ducks."

They start a slow circuit around the duck pond in companionable silence. Jasper continues to mull over Simone's theory of conditional human relations and the unexpected turn of events that has led them to this very conversation in this very park. They linger a while by the pond as Jasper feeds his Coffee Shack biscuit to the ducks. *How about you little critters? How complicated are your feathery little lives?* He wonders.

Halfway around the pond is long enough of a contemplative silence for Simone.

"So, anyway." She elbows Jasper. "Enough of my bleak ramblings. How was your Cognitive coach?"

"Mitch? Yeah, good."

"Come on, Jasper, good's not a good word." She elbows him again gently. "How exactly was he good?"

"He bashed my thinking patterns ferociously as you know, which I've been reflecting on ever since. Despite how raw I felt immediately afterwards, I now realise he did it in such a gracious manner."

"Gracious is better. Gracious how?"

"Well, for all his uncompromising attacks on my unhelpful thinking habits, I never personally felt under attack from him."

"Go on." Simone turns her red gloved hand in a circular motion.

"It was like he scooped my brain from my skull and put it on the table right there between us. He then set about dissecting it, but with me as his assistant."

They walk slowly and deliberately, kicking through thin strips of morning mist hovering over the path.

"I would tell him about some problem or issue troubling me and we would lean over my brain, and he would show me all the connecting thought patterns that interfere with my otherwise healthy thinking – cognitive distortions he called them."

Simone looks up, her brow furrowed. Jasper knows metaphors are not Simone's happy place, but they are his, so he carries on regardless.

"It was like a big lab experiment to reshape the inside of my head. Not jabbing the scalpel at me as such, just my thinking. It felt like he was inviting me on an expedition around the loopy contours of my own brain and reshaping it in the process. We were explorers poking around a dark, quiet interior, where it transpires, there do indeed be dragons." Jasper snatches a look at Simone to see if she's picking up on his metaphor. Nothing. "And I think those dragons might need a little bit of tending to," he says. "I'm just not sure yet whether that means slaying 'em or taming 'em. But they need tending all the same."

Simone taps her chin with her empty cup.

Unable to interpret this exact body language, Jasper continues. "Point is, Mitch made the whole thing feel like a voyage of discovery, not a freak show, and that's no mean feat. To dissect someone's grey matter yet leave them feeling intact and not like they've been under the knife, that's nicely done. So, when our time was up, I plopped my brain back in its housing, shook him by the hand and headed off. It was a bit tender having its useless fatty bits messed with, but all the healthier for it, I think. That's what I mean by gracious."

Simone walks alongside silently. Though far more literal in her thinking, Simone seems to be gradually tuning into Jasper's way of communicating. Spending time with him may help her grapple with her own existential material being stirred up by the coaching.

Issues that always dwell in the infuriatingly abstract shades of grey, somewhere between black and white.

"So, what's the verdict on the Existential coach, Yared, then?" She asks.

"I think his accent is definitely the part," Jasper says. "What is he, Dutch? Austrian? He certainly sounds Freudian. How was he for you?"

Simone never gives platitudes, always searching for the right words. She twice kicks a frozen pinecone along the path before answering. "Ethereal. That's how I'd describe Yared."

"Ethereal," Jasper repeats, taking over pinecone duties. "That beats both gracious and good. Talk to me about ethereal then."

"We just seemed to talk in that other-worldly way I mentioned the other day. Our conversation seemed to transcend the day-to-day and move to another plane altogether. We talked of meanings and values and the purpose and paradox of life. Seriously, the paradox of life! Not a mention of work plans or time and task management or anything like that. It seemed an invitation to move above all that daily stuff to a different level altogether. I never get the chance to have those kinds of conversations, and he seemed just the right person to be having them with, so I took him up on his invitation – wholeheartedly."

Jasper nods and smiles. *Good on you.*

"I don't know exactly what it's achieved yet, but I relished being on that higher plane just for a while. Above the office, above the firm, above the job. Thinking big thoughts about big things. Not a place I naturally gravitate towards, but what a stupefying change of pace and focus."

They exchange glances as they make way for two ornamental poodles to pass by with their equally ornamental walker.

"And how was it for you?" Simone asks, as they resume their stroll.

"Well, if I have a happy place, I think it's definitely up there in those wispy clouds of abstraction. I personally think up there is often more real than our day-to-day slumber down here."

"Slumber?" repeats Simone.

"It's what we do, isn't it? We lumber and slumber. We don't move purposely through life but sleepwalk a lot of the time. But not with Yared. He invites and challenges you to think big. Not just the usual *what* and *how* but the *why* too. Always with the why. It's bloody marvellous. He creates a space where we can ponder these things. Where else can we do that, Simone?" He stops and faces her with hunched shoulders and upturned palms. "Where else, seriously?"

"Seriously?" Simone asks.

"Seriously."

"Here," she says.

"Here?" Jasper looks around the park, confused.

"I say we commit to total honesty while we're on this journey together. We leave behind the daily dullness. We're not polite or superficial. Here we talk one hundred percent openly and only about things of genuine concern. Not news or sport or politics or any other BS. Just important stuff – human stuff. Yes? Deal or no deal?"

"Serious?"

"Serious. Deal or no deal?"

Jasper pulls off a woolly glove and extends his hand. "Damn right, deal."

NEXT TRIP TO the coffee shop and as Simone places down two hot mugs she looks up. *Uh-oh, he doesn't look a happy bunny.*

"Hey, Jasper, how was your gestalt-ing?" she asks, as he joins her.

"Didn't like it," he responds, sitting down and folding his arms.

"How come?"

"It was uncomfortable and pointless. And yes, I know that if it was uncomfortable, it probably did have a point, I'm learning that much at least. But I still didn't like it."

Simone raps her spoon over Jasper's knuckles. "Any experiments?"

"Yep, and similar to yours," Jasper says, licking cold froth off his knuckles. "The coach kept getting me to focus inwards. Not on my thoughts or ideas or any grand philosophy of life, but about how I was feeling. And not even emotional feeling. I've come to even enjoy poking around there, but physical feelings – like bodily sensations."

In a bid to lighten his mood, Simone places a hand on Jasper's and enquires, in the best earnest counselling voice she can muster, "And how was that for you?"

"Bloody uncomfortable is how that was for me. I thought I was getting to grips with this self-exploration stuff. What's in my head and my heart and all that. But this was asking me to explore what's in my body. What sensations I'm experiencing as I'm talking." Jasper's fingers and feet tap simultaneously.

To add to Jasper's woes, today's coffee shop soundtrack once again booms with harsh-edged clanging and banging.

Still in faux-counsellor mode, Simone says, "I can't

help noticing how your feet and fingers are tapping, Jasper. What does that say?"

"Sod off is what that says," Jasper says curtly. "Sorry. Maybe I'll go for decaf next." He looks around restlessly. "I've always lived life in my head. That's my sunny place. But over the years I've learnt to tune in more to my feelings and see them as a legitimate, valid source of data, and that's fine, but now? Now I'm supposed to ask my body what it thinks is going on. As an Indian friend of mine says when a cricket umpire makes a call against his team – '*What the bloody fuck?*'" He kicks away the chair he's been resting his foot on. "Can we talk about something else for the minute?"

"Sure, of course." Simone returns to her normal voice. *He is definitely not a happy bunny.* "Want to hear something funny?"

"Very much," Jasper says, sounding relieved.

"To quote my Cognitive coach from earlier – he thinks my life is as it is because of the *tyranny of my shoulds.*"

"And to quote my Indian friend again, '*What the bloody…?*'"

"Indeed. Apparently, I live my life by a very long list of *shoulds* that I've amassed throughout my life."

"Again, '*What the…?*'"

"You've been through the brain-bashing of the cognitive coaching, haven't you? Didn't you cover the plague of the *shoulds*?" Simone asks.

"Let me see. We bashed my cognitive distortions and thinking errors. Seems I think in quite extreme *black-and-white* terms and not enough in nuanced shades of grey. I mind-read too, convinced I know what others are thinking, and, of course, it's seldom anything positive. I *fortune-tell* also, knowing exactly what will come of that *mind-reading*. And the cherry on top is that I *catastrophise*, bringing all this to an unfounded cataclysmic conclusion. All in a nice rational days' work, eh? But no, we didn't discuss any tyrannical *shoulds*."

"Well, if you think the cognitive coach is tough, check out Albert Ellis on YouTube. The coach told me about him. He's the godfather of a particular cognitive coaching called Rational Emotive Behavioural Coaching. What a character, assertive to the extreme, borderline aggressive I'd say."

Simone notices that Jasper's extremities are now still and he's listening attentively.

"Uncle Albert's theory is that we absorb a whole litany of these *shoulds* as we're growing up. From our parents, our family and our social environments: schools, communities, churches and so on. This all then becomes our default operating code."

"Sounds intriguing," Jasper says. "We're back into brain domain now. Go on."

"We go about our lives as usual, no problem. We *like* this and *prefer* that and that's all fine. But we develop some beliefs and expectations that become completely unconditional, and we cling on to them no matter what. They're not flexible preferences or wishes, they're full-blown, rigid, non-negotiable, demanding *shoulds*. And when they're not met, or they're violated, we go crazy." Simone looks over Jasper's shoulder. "Case in point, see the woman and kids behind you?"

Jasper rolls his eyes, "Can't see 'em, but I can certainly hear 'em."

"Exactly. And it's been irritating me the whole time we've been sitting here too. And while I get continually wound up by them, I can literally hear the rollcall of *shoulds* in my head; she *shouldn't* let her kids run around the coffee shop, she *should* keep them under control, they *shouldn't* be so noisy, they *should* be better behaved – *should, should, should!* And I'm making myself agitated over it too. I'll say it's her and her kids that are making me annoyed, but I now realise that it's me making myself agitated. If I'm that upset about it, I could go over there and politely ask her to control her kids. But, of course, I won't. I'll just sit here, stewing in my own *shoulds*, getting more and more riled about it."

Jasper tuts. "Yeah, but they really, really *should* be more considerate in a coffee shop, *shouldn't* they?"

They both stifle a laugh.

"That's the whole point though, isn't it?" Simone continues. "I happen to agree with you but *why* should they? You and I think they should because this is our refuge from the office where we can talk about this personal stuff, but that's us. For her this is probably a refuge-from-home-and-school. A welcome no-man's-land where she can take a breather from all her other commitments and pressures. She can take a moment for herself and let her kids move about knowing they're perfectly safe and going nowhere. This is a haven for her and a playground for her kids. Meanwhile, it's some sort of bizarre psychiatric antechamber for us. That's what gets us uptight: our reaction and response to how we demand things should be."

"OK then, Miss Alberta Ellis." Jasper straightens up. "Are you saying that the loss and anger, the bereavement, pitifulness and overall general shittiness I felt when my dad left was not because he left, but because I simply thought he *shouldn't* have?"

Oh God, I didn't see that coming. Simone shifts in her

seat. "Of course not," she says, quickly, "but your mum had a choice, didn't she? About how she reacted, I mean."

Jasper looks on with a raised brow.

"When all that happened, you were just a child, weren't you, and at the mercy of childlike reactions. But as an adult, your mother was more in control of her thoughts and emotions and how she chose to perceive and react to things. So, she made a choice. In facing the discovery of her husband living a duplicitous life she chose a calm and reasoned reaction, one that would keep you and her safe in the time ahead."

Well done, Simone, that was nice and clumsy. "Sorry, Jasper. I don't mean to lecture."

"No, you're fine, I get it." He pulls at his chin like he's straightening a beard he doesn't have. "That's a megaton of self-determination and self-responsibility right there." he says, under his breath.

"I know," Simone replies in an apologetic tone.

An age passes then Jasper pulls his chair forward. "So, tell me about all your *shoulds* then, Miss Andersen."

Simone blows out her cheeks. *That's fair.* "They're legion. Where to begin? I can hear and see them clear as day when I'm in all these god-awful boring meetings. I scroll up and down them like a Twitter feed."

Jasper invites the list to be read through the telepathic power of his wrinkled forehead.

Simone puffs out another sigh and begins to recite her menu. "These meetings *shouldn't* be so boring; my colleagues *shouldn't* be such Gekkos; I *shouldn't* have to sit through this tedium every week; I *should* be doing something more meaningful with my life; my life and career *should* have taken a different course; I *should* have made different choices; I *should* have been braver."

Jasper stares across the table. "Bloody 'ell, Simone, that is a shedload-of-*shoulds*. Do you really believe all that?"

"Yep." Simone knots the life out of an already twisted napkin as she nods and wells up. "Bloody Ellis, you mean," she blurts out in a choked laugh.

IN THE COFFEE shop on their final day, Jasper and Simone assume their usual table by the front window. Jasper sips his coffee, looks at Simone and gets straight down to the personal.

"So, tell me about Mr Simone," he says.

Simone looks up, slightly startled. "Can't, I'm afraid."

"Because?"

"Because he waits for me in a part of my future yet to arrive."

"Oh, OK," Jasper says, surprised. "Anyone on the Mr Simone apprenticeship programme then?"

"For a dull girl like me? No."

"No boyfriend?"

"Nope." Simone shifts in her seat. "How about you?"

"Well, I was wondering about Jose, the neighbour's pool boy, but I'm not convinced he's boyfriend material."

"No, you pillock, girlfriend?"

Well, I brought that on myself I suppose – confession time again. "Sort of, kind of," Jasper says.

"Kind of sort of?"

"I was going to give you a platitude and say, 'It's

complicated', but actually it's not. It's perfectly straightforward. We spend time together but live apart at different ends of the country. Different countries actually, she's in Scotland and I'm down here. So, we get together whenever the cosmos aligns. Whenever the stars bless us through their earthly manifestations of seminars and conferences and other such galactic alignments."

Simone looks over. "Wow, your ma really did a number on you with her poetry and philosophy, didn't she?"

Jasper splutters the top off his latte and jerks forward to stop it landing in his lap. "Plus, long weekends and holidays, of course."

"So, you have a floozy up north who you get together with now and then. Like port and storm?"

"I think that's a somewhat uncharitable interpretation," Jasper says, half seriously.

"You're right, I'm sorry. That was out of order."

Jasper shrugs. "She lives near Ullapool and her name's Flo."

"Flo?" Simone laughs reflexively. "Who's actually called Flo these days?"

"Well, Flo is. As in Florence, as in Florence and the Machine."

"You're going out with a pop star?"

"Nooo, just a namesake. Although she does have a similar red-head Medusa thing going on – very wild."

Simone looks over and asks hesitantly, "Is she, er ... single?"

Jasper tunes straight in. "Totally. No family in tow whatsoever."

Simone breathes a sigh.

"She's got a pretty idyllic existence up there, as it happens. She lives in a croft. In a croft? On a croft?

Anyway, it's a tiny cottage and smallholding a mile outside Ullapool that's been in her family since forever. She installed one of Space X's satellite systems and works there as a freelance editor while tending a few fields and assorted bunch of critters. It's a bit of a faff to get to, but you feel seriously off-grid while you're up there." Jasper smiles to himself. "Despite the humongous Starlight Wi-Fi dish bolted to the outhouse."

Simone makes a mental note of a hundred things to ask at some point and then brings the subject back closer to home. "Sounds nice. Tell me though, I've been wondering, how did you find out about your dad?"

Jasper looks up, surprised at the abrupt change of topic. "Er ... he told us. He turned up one evening and just let it all out. Now we have the inside track and the new lingo, I'd say he was having an existential crisis. He realised he wasn't living an honest, authentic life and decided to do something about it. So, he told us, but chose them."

"But your mum took it reasonably well, didn't she?"

"Astonishingly OK. As you said the other day, she must have channelled her inner poet and philosopher. I was also thinking about that Ellis bloke and his 'shoulds' and it reminded me of a stoic philosopher Mum used to quote at me. Ever heard of Epictetus?"

"Vaguely. Durham was a long time ago."

"So was Ancient Greece. Anyway, Epictetus used to say we're not disturbed by things themselves but by the view we take of them. I guess Mum chose a particular view of things that wouldn't leave her poleaxed for the rest of her days. Me, I wanted to kill him. But I was only fifteen and just heading out into the world so figured murder wouldn't make the most auspicious CV entry."

Simone taps the table with a finger like she's trying to remember something. "Sinead O'Connor," she suddenly says.

"Sorry?"

"That sounds like that serenity prayer Sinead O'Connor recites on one of her albums. *"Give us the wisdom to change what we can and accept what we can't."*

"Exactly."

They sit quietly.

"Talking of music, have you heard Pink Floyd's 'Time'?" Jasper asks.

"Like Monsieur Jean-Paul, a bit before my time."

"Maybe, but classics are classics, no? Anyway, it's a nice little existential ditty about the meaninglessness of life, and how it just ticks past, how we waste our time living life in an *offhand way*. There's something frighteningly banal about that phrase for me – living life in an offhand way."

"Cheery," says Simone.

"Yeah, but that's the existential stuff, isn't it? Not bleak or depressing in its own right, it just forces you to look at your own choices and decisions. And question whether you're spending your time authentically ... or in an *off-hand way*. Roger Waters, Britain's own contemporary existentialist, who'd have thought it?"

Another reflective moment passes then suddenly Jasper kicks Simone's ankle. "Look lively, Simone. Here comes bloody Liam."

Liam weaves his way through the coffee shop clientele to their table. "How we doing folks?" he asks with a toothy smile and sits down.

"Er ... we're OK. What are you doing here?" asks

Simone suspiciously.

"Just passing," Liam says. "How on earth did you find this place?"

"We chose it for its obscure back-street charm, Liam. So, you're not just passing, are you. What's up?"

"You're right." He grins. "Well, a couple of things. First off, how's the coaching going? Are you getting anything from it?"

Silence.

"Simone?"

"Yes, I am, actually," she replies guardedly.

"How so?" Liam crosses his arms and legs.

"Well, it seems to be helping me work out what motivates and engages me. It's helping me understand what I value, in my work and in my career. That sort of thing."

"You know I could've helped you with all that, you only needed to ask," Liam says facetiously.

Simone just runs a finger across her forehead and moves her fringe behind her ear.

"How about you, Jasper, you a new man yet?" He turns to Jasper.

"Nearly."

"Seriously, is it helping?" Liam presses.

"Well, seriously then, yes, it is. It's helping me with my cognitive restructuring among other things."

Liam leans back. "Your what?"

"It's helping me think about my thinking. A kind of cerebral spring clean if you will."

"Jolly good. That should all sound suitably impressive in the evaluation report."

An awkward moment follows then Simone interjects, "You said there were a couple of things?"

"Right, yes." Liam places his palms on the table.

"You know the researcher from the university who instigated this coaching? Well, it turns out he's coaching her upstairs too. You may or may not know this, but like you guys, she and I started at the firm together about a thousand years ago. I love her dearly, but I've never seen anything like it before. It's like she's found religion. She says her personal experience of the coaching is so profound she wants to introduce it down through the rank and file."

"Great idea, but what does that have to do with us?" Jasper asks.

"Well, she wants to begin by training up a couple of managers as internal coaches. And because you guys have started the process, I thought you're as good a place to start as any. What do you think?"

Simone and Jasper look blankly at Liam. "What do we think about what?"

"What do you think about training up as coaches?" Liam smiles.

They continue their blank stares.

"OK. You don't have to answer me now, just have a think about it." He slides over two business cards. "This fella runs his business out of Cumbria and his next training programme starts in July. You've got the OK to join it if you want to."

They both study the cards. *'Devoke Consulting. Dr Al Wainwright – Head of Coaching.'*

"Al Wainwright?" Jasper exclaims. "Are you kidding?"

Liam and Simone look over.

"Albert Wainwright, seriously?" Jasper repeats.

Blank stares.

Liam breaks the confusion. "I don't know if it's Albert, Alfred, or Alli Baba to be honest. Have a think and let me know. If you decide you want to go ahead, you're free to contact him direct. Just update me either way."

Simone looks questioningly again at Jasper. 'Wainwright?' she mouths.

"Don't worry about it. Google him. If his parents come from up there, they sure have a sense of humour, that's all I'll say."

"OK, I'll leave you to it." Liam stands up and pushes his chair under the table. "See you back in the office." He heads towards the door, leaving Jasper and Simone studying Dr Wainwright's business cards.

"Whaddya think?" asks Jasper.

"I'm in." Simone says.

"Serious? Just like that? You don't need to sleep on it?"

"Nope," Simone responds emphatically. "I've learnt so much about myself in these few brief coaching conversations, I'm sold. And if I've learnt so much from having these conversations, why would I not want more of that, and, even better, learn to do it myself?" Simone flicks the business card with a fingernail. "So, yes, I'm in. How about you?"

"If you're in, then I'm in," Jasper says. "Besides…" he taps his business card on Simone's to make a toast "…it's way too early to break up the band"

Chapter Two
COACHING, LIFE AND THE LAKES

"Nice place," Simone shouts.

"I know, I was lucky to get it," Jasper shouts back, from two floors up. "How do you afford Hampstead on your salary?"

"Well, technically it's Highgate and it is only rented. Mind out." A black holdall flies over the balcony and thumps to the ground next to her. "Are we taking yours or mine?"

"Don't mind." Simone grabs the bag.

"OK, stick it in the boot of mine, would you? It's behind yours." Jasper throws the keys down onto the grass. "I'll lock up and be down."

Simone loads the bags into Jasper's boot and leans against the car to take in his new flat. *A mock Tudor apartment in NW7. What I wouldn't give.* She thinks. *Trees and shrubs, I can smell the green. Something vaguely resembling a view and if I'm not mistaken even some oxygen in the air.* She looks around, nodding at the trimmed hedges, ornate iron railings and black Victorian streetlights. *Very nice.*

She notices a mass of crumpled dark clothes shuffling along the path. As it passes by a grubby face appears from below a tattered old trilby, and a toothless mouth curls into a grin. A nicotine-stained finger taps the peak, "Morning, ma'am."

"Er ... erm ... yes, good morning."

The face disappears, and the mass moves on.

"Who's your friend?" Jasper suddenly appears with a rucksack over his shoulder. "Oh, you know, just making friends with your neighbours." She climbs into the passenger side. "Even your transient folk are polite up here."

"Ha! He's not transient, that's Hobo-Joe. He's got himself a very nice shack over on the heath. Lovely old bloke."

Simone smiles at him as they drive past but he doesn't look up.

"So, three hundred miles and six hours. I trust you've brought the music, the snacks and the address," Jasper says as they join the North Circular.

"Well–" Simone rummages in her shoulder bag and pulls out a bag of seed mix and a bruised banana. "—I've got snacks ... of sorts."

Jasper glances over. "Right, so that'll be a burger stop at the services then. Music?"

She waves her folding Galaxy with a connection lead wrapped around it.

"Excellent. Address?"

"From memory–" Simone closes her eyes. "—Abbey House, Edendale Head, Cumbria. CA20 something, something, something. I've got it on my phone."

"Excellent." Jasper tilts his head back onto the headrest. "Dr Wainwright ... here we come."

Three hundred miles and seven slow hours pass, and they arrive in deep west Cumbria. Jasper stops the car at the mouth of the valley and turns the engine off. They peer out of the windscreen into the evening gloom.

"Are we sure about this?" whispers Jasper.

They sit quietly, staring down the valley as the

mountains stare back.

"I am," Simone eventually says.

Jasper nods silently.

"You see that peak at the end?" Simone nods towards every mountain in view.

"Er, yeah."

"I'm going to climb that before we leave," she says.

"Really?"

"Yep."

"Why?" Jasper looks over.

"I feel it in my bones, Jasper. Something's beckoning me down this valley, and I don't think I'll be leaving quite the same as I enter. And climbing that peak will be an important part of it."

"Because?"

"Because…" Simone does a drum roll on the dashboard "…that's where I'm finally going to bury Miss Andersen."

"You're going to bury her on top of a mountain?"

"Yep."

"Fair enough." Jasper restarts the engine. "Best we get down there then."

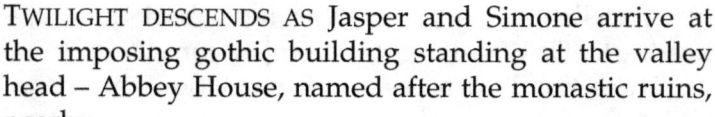

TWILIGHT DESCENDS AS Jasper and Simone arrive at the imposing gothic building standing at the valley head – Abbey House, named after the monastic ruins, nearby.

Wow, Jasper thinks.

They crunch across the gravel drive to the colossal oak door. Above it a faded coat of arms just about reads – *E Glande Quercus*.

"From the acorn, the Oak," Simone translates as

they walk under it.

"We'll see about that," Jasper mutters as he shoves open the enormous oak door and tiptoes through.

"Hi folks, welcome. I'm Al Wainwright and you guys are?" Alan says, waving them straight into the grand hall.

"Jasper Oran."

"Simone Marshall."

"Great to meet you both. Let me get you a drink." Looking strangely out of place in his dark three-piece suit, Al walks over to an immense dark sideboard stacked with ailing crockery. "We've got tea, green tea, fruit tea or coffee. Espresso, Americano or Latte."

"Latte, please," Simone replies.

"Same, please." Jasper strolls into the central hall to the huge fireplace carved into the main wall. He looks around wide-eyed at the acres of wood paneling and faded oil paintings.

Simone plonks herself on one of the huge couches in front of the fireplace with its coffin-sized grate. She takes in their new surroundings, their home from home for the coming week.

"Here you go, two lattes." Al places a tray down on the low coffee table. "How was your journey up?"

"Absolutely fine." Jasper stretches for his coffee. "Until we took the shortcut over Hardknott Pass."

"Ah, yes, that can focus the attention somewhat." Al flashes a smile.

"You're not kidding." Jasper laughs. "London doesn't prepare you for that. Nothing more challenging than the Blackwall Tunnel and the Dartford Crossing." He points his thumb over his shoulder. "On the way down, we passed some ruins off to the side. What was that?"

"Hardknott Roman Fort. Well worth a visit if you

like piles of old bricks," Al says. Simone looks nonplussed, but Jasper smiles. "I do indeed like piles of old bricks."

"You have a morning off midweek, so if it's not tipping down with rain that might be an option." Al wanders over to stoke the blazing fire. "Excuse the formal attire, I'm just back from a posh corporate do in Kendal."

"That's a relief, I was concerned we may be somewhat underdressed," Simone says. "So, what do you have in store for us this week, Al?"

"Lots of wonderful stuff," he replies. "You'll leave here a different person, I guarantee it."

Simone flashes Jasper a piercing stare that he interprets as *I told you so!*

"Anyway, more of all that in the morning. For now, here's the brief orientation." Al walks over to the windows and starts pulling together the long thick red velvet curtains. He points out the window. "The fell to the side is just a hundred metres high and a nice gentle toddle before breakfast if you're an early riser. Fell to the back is steeper and higher, so takes longer. But you've got the light this time of year, so it can be a pleasant option for the end of the day if you still have the energy."

He points towards a dark tract next to the grand staircase. "Through there is the kitchen and canteen where you feed yourselves. If you want someone else to feed you, then there's the Abbey Inn a few hundred yards back up the lane. And if you like real ale, you can get my namesake up there too – a cracking pint of Wainwrights."

"So, who was this Wainwright fellow exactly?" asks Simone.

"Local legend – though no relative, unfortunately.

I'd probably get discounted ale if he was." Al continues his orientation. "From across the lane you can follow the river in both directions.' He points one way. "Keep going right and you'll hit the village, the main road and eventually the Irish Sea." He points the other way. "Keep going left and you'll find Eden Water. If you then keep going beyond that, you'll eventually get to the top of Eden Fell, about six hundred metres. Higher than the pass you came over so quite a commitment if you're thinking about it."

Simone and Jasper listen quietly, continuing to take in the house's faded grandeur.

Jasper studies the rooms architecture. *When did they stop building places this, mighty and noble? When did they stop bothering to make high arched doorways and windows of lead and stone and three feet deep?*

"Who else do we have joining us, Al?" Simone breaks the silence.

"We've got a good turnout actually. So good, in fact, we're running the training in two different groups. One group will work with me in there." He nods to a large, paneled door at the far end of the hall. "The other group will be in a room just off the landing upstairs. My partner in crime, Alison, will be running that one."

"So, Al and Al?" Jasper says. "That's neat."

"Correct. And word to the wise…" Al leans forward and lowers his tone. "I'm the good cop."

An acre of panels reverberates with laughter.

"Alison is great, you'll love her. She's coming over from Carlisle in a couple of hours, so you might get to meet her later. Also, we've taken the liberty of splitting you guys up. We find it's a richer experience for friends and co-workers to join different groups. It helps them see different styles and hear different voices, etcetera. Hope that's OK."

"After hours in the car with this guy, that's more than OK." Simone laughs.

"Likewise," Jasper says.

"You'll both be in good company, anyway. We've a solid mix of consultant coaches, independent coaches, and internal coaches much like yourselves."

"Hear that?" Jasper throws a threadbare cushion at Simone. "We're gonna be coaches!"

AT THE END of the first day Simone and Jasper wander to the pub for a drink and a debrief.

The solid granite Abbey Inn would look dour and foreboding on the village green in middle England but at the valley head it looks the perfect local hostelry: brutish and thick walled but welcoming enough on its own terms. Above the entrance a blanched sign swings on a creaking frame and Friar Tuck stares down looking more like a fat pig in sandals and bathrobe.

The heavy clack of the iron latch ricochets around the empty bar as they enter. Its stone walls covered in old-fashioned climbing garb along with black-and-white photos of the old wiry characters who used to climb locally.

Simone heads straight to the bar under a heavy-beamed low ceiling and is confronted with a bewildering array of hand pumps. "What are you drinking from this lot Jasper?"

"A pint of our course leader's namesake, please."

Simone orders a gin and tonic and pint of Wainwrights and follows Jasper through a low stone doorway to the garden. They emerge onto a manicured lawn dotted with tatty white metal furniture. Simone walks towards a table in the center gazing up silently at the surrounding fells bathed in early evening apricot. She pulls out a heavy iron chair. "Growing up in the shadow of Heathrow, I just didn't know this sort of place existed in England, did you?"

"Well, we went to the Peak District once as a kid, but I was far too young for it to make much of an impression." Jasper takes a gulp of ale. "You must have had some good scenery up in Durham, surely?"

Simone thinks back. "Beaches were amazing and there was some nice moorland. But nothing on this scale. Look at it."

"Keep heading north into Scotland, and up near Florence it gets even crazier," Jasper says.

"This will do me for now, I think." Simone sips her G & T, staring up at the silhouetting skyline.

"By the way," Jasper says after a while. "You know the peak you want to chuck Miss Andersen off? Well, I checked on the wall map in the reading room. Guess how high it is."

"Hmm, a mile high?" Simone randomly suggests.

Jasper gets out his phone and does some sums. "Nope, half that – eight hundred metres."

"Easy-peasy," she says.

"Hah! Well, we'll see about that, won't we?"

"We? Are you coming up with me then?"

"'Course I am. I baptised Miss Andersen after all, so it's only fitting I'm there at her burial." Jasper raises his glass.

"Sky burial," Simone says.

"I'm sorry, sky burial?"

"Yes, it is a thing, you know."

Jasper shrugs.

"I read about it in *National Geographic*. It happens a

lot up on the high plateaus in Central Asia, Tibet, places like that. They leave bodies on piles of rocks to be blown dry by the cold wind and picked clean by the birds. I think it's quite a dignified way to go, somehow. Better than rotting in the damp earth – depressing. Or burnt to a cinder and ground up – brutal. Miss Andersen should think herself lucky she's getting such a dignified send-off after the dull life she's chained me to."

"Fair enough." Jasper sips his drink, scanning the jagged hilltops. "So, what was happening in your group today?"

"Alison got us started upstairs with listening and empathy."

"And?"

"Listening is a strange one, isn't it?" Simone begins. "In effect, all you have to do is keep quiet and pay attention. But this most simple act seems maddeningly difficult for most of us. We always seem to want to invite ourselves into other people's thoughts, trespassing with our own ideas and advice. Always with the advice. 'You should do it this way' or 'I would do it that way'. I see it all the time in the office, and I hate it. It's so disrespectful and unhelpful when you're trying to figure something out for yourself. Why do we do it?" Simone stabs her straw into her drink.

"I blame the Greeks," Jasper says, flatly.

"Funny."

"No, seriously. You did Classics, you should know. They basically set the tone for Western thought, and it was all about, truth, logic and debate. So, we tend not to naturally explore when we're in discussion with someone, even these days. We just advise or say what we think is right or logical. Pretty limiting really – adversarial even. Definitely not what this coaching lark is all about."

Simone taps the straw on the end of her nose. "No, it really isn't. It makes you realise just how one-dimensional our normal work communication is, doesn't it? Shallow, counterproductive, and disingenuous a lot of the time. We don't seem to genuinely listen to each other. We all just jostle and posture and try to outdo each other to look good or sound good." She zips up her fleece.

Jasper also folds up his collar against the gathering wind. "Getting chilly, shall we go in."

Simone leads them back inside, around a group of earthy locals assembled at the bar discussing valley-matters, and towards a large wood burner in the corner.

Simone sits cross-legged on the decrepit old leather couch, immediately hypnotised by the stove's orange glow. "Do you know," she says as Jasper tries to get comfortable on his half of the couch. "I think I can count on one hand the number of real fires or stoves I've sat in front of. They're bloody amazing."

"Yeah, they are." Jasper says. "Happiest childhood memories I have are sitting in front of the living room fire. To be five again, eh?"

Simone sits quiet and content in front of the warm stove in the middle of nowhere, thrilled by her newfound ability to enjoy the uncertain and the unknown of what lies ahead and to be on another coaching journey from here to who-knows-where.

"I'm starting to hear a few swear words slip off your tongue there, Simone. What's that about?" Jasper says breaking her reverie.

"Well, as Miss Andersen wasn't much for swearing, I thought I might try out some more colourful language."

"What's brewing, Simone? You def sound like a woman on the turn if you'll pardon the expression."

"I think I am." She doesn't move an inch. "Something's shifting all right. It started with the coaching in London, and I think this training, in this place, is all part of it. I'm already bored at the prospect of going back to work." She blinks at the stove. "Something's emerging, Jasper, and I really don't think it's going to find expression in all those sodding PowerPoint presentations I seem to spend my life in. There you go, there's another cuss." She laughs.

"Excellent." Jasper puts his feet up on the edge of a large wicker log basket.

"Anyway," Simone says, "what did your group do behind the big-paneled door today?"

Jasper places his glass on the stone floor and then leans back into the couch. "We mainly spent the morning looking at different coaching definitions and exploring the difference between coaching and counselling."

"Pray tell."

"They use a lot of similar skills clearly, like the questioning and active listening and that. But Al was explaining how the energy and focus is fundamentally different in coaching. It's much more future-focused and goal-orientated. On the face of it, it's about improving performance, finding solutions to challenges, achieving goals and what have you. But it's far more than that. It's also about facilitating self-directed learning and growth, fostering a person's sense of self-responsibility and what he calls 'agency'. Pretty deep stuff it seems."

They sit listening to the crackling stove.

"I got a real sense of that from the sessions we did with our own coaches," Simone says. "I started experiencing some real shifts even when not talking directly about work issues or performance goals."

"We also covered a variety of coaching models with different acronyms," Jasper continues in a slightly bored tone as he reaches down to retrieve his drink.

"We did those, too. You don't sound too impressed."

"They're OK. Interesting to see how you can use them to structure a meaningful conversation that achieves something rather than one that just rambles around. They are what they are, I guess. Just techniques to keep you focused and moving forward."

He picks a piece of kindling from the basket and starts peeling off the bark. "We also explored what it means to be *present*, which seems as important as having a roadmap or a good question up your sleeve. More so perhaps. People sharing their deep personal stuff really need to be heard. Talking it through and feeling heard can help them make sense of what's swimming around their heads."

He looks around and sees no one else looking like they will do the honours, so he takes a log from the basket and tips it into the stove.

"But they need a skilled listener, one who can offer reactions to what they're hearing in the moment. That can be powerful. Maybe even the principal thing the coach can offer. When I think back to our own coaching, there was a lot of that going on, particularly with the Gestalt coach. Or saintly-Lorna, I remember you calling her. Some were doing it different to others, but they were all absolutely present all the time, weren't they?"

"One hundred percent," Simone says.

Jasper continues, "We seem to live in this fun-house hall of mirrors, obsessed with what others think of us and what we think of what they think. It's an infinite loop of madness. The reality is that we're all so self-obsessed we rarely dwell on anyone else too much anyway, only as reflections of ourselves."

The group of locals has swollen considerably and loud guffaws bellow from the bar.

"To have a professional just sit there and listen. No judgement. No prejudice. No advice. How powerful is that?" Jasper goes on. "Helping you hear more clearly what's what. What you know, think you know, want to know, and don't know. It's like your own echo chamber has some acoustic cladding stuck onto the walls absorbing all the reverberations and distortions. It becomes quiet and still. You start to hear yourself think, finally."

"You're right." Simone watches the spitting stove and ponders how seldom she experiences such meaningful presence or dialogue at work. She looks over her shoulder at the bar. "It's getting a bit lively in here. Shall we head back and see what magic we can work in that antique microwave?"

DAY TWO AND Jasper is up at first light, heading for the abbey ruins. He turns a corner in the lane and comes across some moss-covered footings just a metre high. *Well, they could've been anything. A church, a house, a medieval knocking shop.* Then he turns another bend. "Now that's an abbey."

Jasper is a fan of old bricks, and this is a mighty fine pile. The business end of the abbey ruins still stands over fifteen metres tall, largely intact, around what would have been the central nave. The rising sun slices through the upper reaches as he studies the hollowed-out structure, reflecting on what life must have been like in the 1100s.

The monks who inhabited this place must have been the coaches and counsellors of their day. Listening to everyone's concerns and confessions, bearing witness, offering redemption and solace. Why would they build a place like this here though, so remote? Maybe that was the point: to keep the confessions cloistered and closeted. He blows into the mist, walking among the twenty-feet-high arched stone cloisters. *Stone bones standing for a thousand years, with the Romans here a thousand years before that. Forts and abbeys for defence and deference.* He wanders aimlessly through the ruins. *What other confessionals will I bear witness to today. And what might I confess myself I wonder.*

Jasper leans back against a lichen-covered inner wall to grasp the abbey's scale. *Whatever they are, I'm sure it won't be anything these walls haven't heard before. They may come with a contemporary twist, but I reckon it'll be the same old human stuff. Hope, fear and confusion.* Jasper studies the intact windows, like sunken eyes still gazing out after a thousand years. *What life they must have seen. What number of inconsequential human dots like me come and go?* He rubs his hands against the morning cold and pulls up his collar. *Enough already – time for porridge.*

"MORNING, MIND IF we join you?" Simone and Jasper hover over Alison and her pink grapefruit.

"Of course not. Please." She pushes aside some crockery to make space.

"These rickety old long benches make this place

look like an old school canteen," Jasper says, placing his tray down.

"That's exactly what it was, until 1939 anyway. The rooms we're training in were the junior boys' dormitories, and the rooms you're sleeping in were the senior boys' study-bedrooms. Then of course everything changed, and in the war, it was a hospital for a time, I think." Alison pushes her grapefruit shell to one side.

"What do you have in store for us today, Alison?" Simone asks, picking at her toast.

"The Transtheoretical Theory of Change," Alison answers, with a slight smirk.

Jasper's teacup stops halfway to his face. *The what?*

"It's a model of behavioural change that will help your coaching clients target specific behaviour change."

"Oh, OK." Jasper's cup continues its journey. "How would you use that then?" Simone asks.

"Well, have either of you ever tried health kicks or New Year's resolutions or anything like that?"

"Sure," says Simone. "I trained for a marathon once."

"I gave up smoking," Jasper adds. "Nearly as impressive, eh?"

"Both great examples." Alison adds a sweetener drop to her tea. "Let's take you, Jasper, how long did you smoke for?"

"Oh, about fifteen years, mid-teens to late twenties."

"And then what happened?"

"Then I saw my uncle get ill with lung problems, and I started to get a bit breathless myself sometimes, so thought it was maybe time to quit."

"And then what happened?"

Jasper realises he's suddenly in the hot seat. "Then I did pretty much nothing about it for another couple of years, other than fret and wonder about whether I should do something about it."

"And then what happened?"

Jasper looks at Simone. *Is she always like this?* Simone just smiles.

"Then what happened, Jasper?"

"Then I decided to go for it, and I set the date, which I'm embarrassed to say was midnight on New Year's Eve.

"And then?"

"Then? Then I gave up."

"Completely?" Alison asks.

"Well, no. It took a couple of years, to be fair." Jasper eyes the peanut butter sandwich in his hand.

"What happened during those couple of years?" Alison raises his sandwich elbow for him.

"Thanks." He takes a small bite. "Then I stayed off the fags for the most part, except for the occasional misdemeanor, you know."

"Like when?"

"Christmas was always a good excuse for a fat cigar. That was a proper reason for a smoke, I thought. But then any occasion became a reason, and it went from occasional big cigars to a pocket-sized pack of cigarillos, ready for any occasion, even just a weekend night out in the end."

"Where are you with it now, Jasper?"

"Now? All good. Clean and green for five years straight." He washes down the last of his tea.

Meanwhile, Alison picks up the overglazed Beatrix Potter teapot and fills everyone's cup.

"And that, my new friends, is a perfect example of transtheoretical change."

"What...? But..." Jasper starts but goes quiet, unsure of what his question is.

"How about you, Simone. How long did you think about doing a marathon?"

"Since forever."

"And how long did you train for it?"

"Just the year before I decided to do It."

"That's a nice intense example."

"Come on, Alison, stop being so coy. What's this trans-theory thing?" Simone taps the teapot with a long fingernail.

"Jasper's is a great example of all the theoretical stages." Alison sips the last of her tea and puts the cup to one side. "You ready?"

Jasper and Simone nod expectantly.

"The stages are as follows: precontemplation, contemplation, preparation, action and maintenance."

They sit silently.

"Jasper said he smoked for fifteen years, and it never crossed his mind to quit. Why should he? There's no reason to. That's *precontemplation*. Then, when his uncle got ill, he started thinking about quitting. Nothing more than thinking about the pros and the cons of it. And he did this for two years. 'Fret and wonder' I think were your own words, Jasper?"

He nods.

"In the precise terms here, that's called *contemplation*, when you start to think about changing whatever it is you're thinking about changing. Follow?"

"Yes," they say in unison.

"Then you move into *preparation*. Finally, the stage when you start mobilising. I imagine this was when you started getting serious about your marathon, Simone. Buying the right gear, mapping out your training route, stuff like that."

"Totally."

"And back to you, Jasper, it's finally time to commit to your nicotine abstinence which you do on New Year's Eve at twelve o'clock. And that, finally, is the *action* stage. Congratulations."

"Er ... OK."

"But that's not the end of it, because you lapse. Of course, you do." She eyes Jasper knowingly.

"It's inevitable, it's human. You have the odd celebratory cigar when you think there's an occasion for it. I'm the same." Alison waves her Stevia sachets. "When I'm in coffee shops, I don't use this, I go full-on brown sugar. But over time I've done it less and less. All part of the change cycle."

"The biggest thing to realise is that it's just lapse and not relapse. The natural last part of the change cycle – *maintenance*. When you're abstaining, Jasper, or when you're out training, Simone, that's not the end of it. Your work here is to make your slips off the wagon, fewer and further between, all on the road to final behaviour change." Alison looks at them both. "Make sense?"

"Sure does, and no wonder so many New Year's resolutions are doomed," Simone says. "We tend to think it's binary; we're on a diet or we're not, we're on a health kick or we're not. Not that simple though by the sounds of it."

"Behaviour change is a complicated business–" Alison gathers her used crockery and winks at Simone. "—as you'll discover this week."

"I THOUGHT I might find you and your Wainwrights out here." Simone wanders through the unkempt

Abbey garden towards Jasper. It's midweek, the height of summer, and every plant, flower and shrub has been left dry to fight for its life.

"They've got a crate of these bad boys in the larder," says Jasper, waving a bottle of ale above his head.

"I could do with one of those actually, I'm knackered." Simone collapses onto a chair.

"Help yourself." Jasper slides an opened full bottle across the table.

"Alison had us practicing the entire day," Simone says.

"Us too. How are you finding it?"

"How am I finding it?" Simone takes a sip of ale and scans the garden for the right words. "Tough, draining, emotional and amazing."

"Yep, and freeing too," Jasper adds.

"I like the sound of that. How so?"

Jasper picks at the label peeling from his bottle.

"I've brought all sorts of things into our coaching practice already, and even just having the conversations with the other trainees is really untangling my thinking. Threads that our own coaching started to pull at, just continue to loosen. And, without wanting to kill the metaphor, as the stitching starts to come away, I become less concerned about keeping things together and more curious about what happens as they come apart."

"This beer isn't quite as yuck as I imagined," Simone says. "So, what are you bringing to be picked at then?"

In an exaggerated professorial tone, Jasper begins. "I've discussed why I'm doing a job I don't enjoy, why I don't enjoy it and what sort of job I might enjoy. All nice easy beginners' stuff for my unsuspecting co-

coach." He looks at Simone's deadpan expression and drops the theatrical tone. "The poor bloke I'm paired up with was like a rabbit in headlights when I dumped that little lot on him. Poor sod." He continues in a more serious tone. "It's astonishing. Like we were saying yesterday, just to talk this stuff through out loud can be a revelation. What did we ever talk about before we talked about the important stuff, Simone?"

Simone purses her lips. *I have absolutely no idea.*

"But as I said yesterday, I could do without the other trainees butting in with their advice. Al's coming down pretty hard on that now. We can't help ourselves, can we? It's like we're programmed just to tell, tell, tell. When it should be listen-ask-repeat. Can't blame them, I suppose. I fall into the same trap. Why it's so difficult to just listen is beyond me. But you feel it when you're on the receiving end of even well-intended advice. It's so jarring." Jasper continues to pick at his soggy beer label. "Anyway, how about you, what are you bringing in?"

"Same sort of stuff." Simone also picks at Jasper's label and starts rolling it into a small pile of soggy balls. "Trying to figure out what a post-Finance world might look like."

"Are you getting any sense of it?"

"None whatsoever. But I suspect this is all part of the process. I also suspect that Liam would be rather peeved if he knew the rough direction of travel this could all be taking."

Jasper nods. "You're not kidding."

"I like talking everything through, that's for sure. It's like you need to throw out your thoughts just to clear the airwaves, get some quieter airspace and listen to what new thoughts come down the channels." She tilts her head to admire her soggy ball pyramid. "Makes you appreciate what the professionals do. But it can be so hard to let people work through their own wishes and woes without injecting your own tuppence-worth."

Jasper takes aim and flicks the neat pyramid off into the grass. "Do you think we'll crack it?"

"I reckon we're made of the right stuff, sure." Simone pinches Jasper's knuckle for ruining her pyramid. "Simply not believing we've got all the answers is a good start and we've got that far at least. Just let grown-up folk do their grown-up thinking, that's the key. Don't infantilise by spoon-feeding or handholding. Walk alongside people as they explore and experiment. Witness their journey wherever it takes them. Just don't give them the co-ordinates. it's their plan, their goal, their journey. Tag along and walk to the edge with them, sure, but don't jump and don't push. Let them take the lead. It's their destiny, after all." *Their decisions and their destiny.* Simone senses she is already making important breakthroughs in her understanding, even this early on.

The entire valley is still and silent except for the bleating lambs.

"Which is exactly what this guy this morning didn't, or couldn't, do, God help him." Jasper shakes his head. "He was trying to wring goals and actions out of me like his life depended on it. He wouldn't just walk alongside me. It was like he was dragging me along on a lead. I know a lot of coaching can be about helping people make progress towards their goals, but sometimes it's just about helping them explore and understand their goals. Are they the real thing? What do their goals mean and what do they represent? Stuff like that."

Jasper sets about another label. "What can help

people is the clarity and understanding that comes from deeply exploring where they're currently at. What's working and what's not. Why and why not. Then genuine goals emerge. It's just that we're never given the chance to talk things through that deeply without being railroaded into premature conclusions or actions by our bosses or colleagues."

"And into predetermined goals," Simone adds.

"Exactly," Jasper continues. "Don't tell me what I should or shouldn't decide on as a goal. Help me explore my existing situation and all its possible alternatives and from that, decisions, actions and goals will emerge. I'm not a flaming idiot. I might at times be confused or unsure about something, even temporarily lost, but I'm not an imbecile. Help me gain clarity on these things and then I'll happily do the rest myself and I won't feel a premature goal or action has been foisted upon me. They'll be my decisions, my goals and my plans."

Simone rests the cold beer bottle on the side of her head while she listens to Jasper's rant, in silence.

"Exactly like you're doing here with me now, Simm. Perfect."

THE REMAINS OF Mediobogdum sit beside the insanely steep Hardknott Pass. A Roman fort built in AD 100 and at eight hundred feet stood the second highest in all Britannia, a site of the highest strategic order. The Pass shields its rear while the front holds the entire valley in its sights. The local Celts were not going to make too many surprise raids here.

"So, whaddya think?" asks Jasper, wandering among the four-foot stone walls.

Simone twists her lips. "I'm not feeling it to be honest, just looks like a pile of old bricks to me."

Jasper shakes his head. "Knowing we were coming up here, and to celebrate the Romans, I swiped a copy of Marcus Aurelius' *Meditations* from the reading room. You've read it, haven't you?"

"We covered it in Classics, but I can't remember much." Simone sits down on a lower wall of what is left of the centurions' granary. "These views are stunning," she mumbles to herself.

The unpredictable sky is low today. Mist tumbles across the fells and swirls around the tops of the nearby bulks. Scafell and Scafell Pike stand shoulder to shoulder making an impenetrable defense to the north, looking glum and indifferent.

Jasper staggers over uneven ground to the far corner with the best view across the valley. A pillar of light breaks through the mist, illuminating the side of Ill Crag and Esk Pike, making their shadowy Scafell kin look even more sullen.

Simone shouts over the wind, "Look at this." She points at a squat rectangle of bricks. "This was the tribune, where they gave out daily orders to the officers. That must be where 'tribunal' comes from. I'm going to throw in that fact when I'm next in one of those godawful meetings."

"Don't do it, Simone," Jasper shouts back. *Don't do it.* "Do what?"

"Bring work into this hallowed place." He gazes up at the rocky drama of Crinkle Craggs breaking through the mist. "I'm fucking dreading going back," he hollers.

"Me too." Simone trudges through the stout brick blocks to join Jasper leaning on his forearms, shoulders slumped. "Then, what on earth are we doing there?" she asks.

"As far as I can tell, I'm wasting my life fiddling with software and metrics and you're dying a slow death in never-ending finance meetings. Like Caesar – but death by a thousand PowerPoints."

"Does Marcus have any wisdom to share with us on this?" Simone asks.

Jasper pulls *Meditations* from his jacket pocket and flicks through the pages. "Nope, nope, nope. Oh, how about this?" He straightens up. "*Soon you will be ashes and bones. A mere name at most. And even that will be just a sound – an echo.*" He stuffs the small book into his jacket and looks around. "Quite apt really. This is most definitely a place of echoes and ghosts."

Simone follows his gaze around the site.

"If we ever return here, Simone, haunting our former selves, I hope to God we've taken some wisdom from Marcus and this place and changed our course." *Before we too are just ashes and bones.*

"Me too." Simone stands with hands in her puffed-out pockets staring down the valley to the sea. "I bet Marcus Aurelius never had a career crisis as emperor."

Jasper again leans on the outer wall and daydreams down into the valley. *A mere name at most. And when the last person who knows that name also dies, then you're truly dead.*

Simone steps alongside and nudges him with her shoulder. "What did you want to be as a kid anyway? Not an IT emperor, I'm guessing."

"Err … the usual, I guess. Astronaut, fireman, cowboy. Even considered long-distance lorry driver at about the age of ten. Mum thought that one was quite romantic. Not now though with all its quotas and schedules and spies in the cab – I think it's about as glamorous as any Amazon delivery job." He turns around to watch some brave souls tackle the Hardknott helter-skelter. "And now I find myself stuck in this pointless daily rut grappling with all the company SLAs and KPIs and what-the-fuck have yous. The glamour and adventure of it all, aye, Simone?"

He shoves her playfully off a turf clump she's balancing on. "How about you? What sage advice did you get from your school careers' emperor?"

"Well—" Simone kicks her boots back against the turf lump. "—first, I wanted to be an architect like my dad, of course, and then a teacher like my mum. All very predictable. Then I disappointed us all by going into corporate finance. I mean, whoever heard of that? What child ever says their grand plan as a grown-up is to go into corporate finance. I mean please."

She steps up onto a small stone footing. "Do you know what Mediobogdum means?"

Jasper looks up and shrugs. "Nope."

"Roughly translated it's 'middle place'."

She knows her languages alright, Jasper thinks.

"And with all this coaching, it's starting to feel like it too, isn't it? A middle place."

"A middle place between what and where?" Jasper asks, squinting through the wind.

"Between...!" Simone suddenly shouts throwing her arms out left and right "... hither and thither and betwixt and between."

Jasper cranes his neck. "I know that place well, Simm. Between *no-more* and *not-yet*. Feels like I've lived there all my life."

She jumps down and lands a hand on Jasper's shoulder. "Any parting wisdom from Marcus before we leave the old boneyard?"

He pulls out *Meditations* again and thumbs

through. "How about this one?" He holds the book aloft. "'*Whatever happens to you has been waiting to happen to you since the beginning of time.*' Time and fate conjoined. How about that?"

Simone thinks for a moment, then pats her stomach through her luminescent yellow jacket. "I think fate, time and hunger have all conjoined and are taking us back down. C'mon Aurelius Oran ... time for cream tea."

NEXT EVENING SIMONE is wandering the gloomy house corridors on a roundabout route back to her room. She passes an old, faded charcoal picture of a young nun in prayer and stops to study it. *Look at you, so solemn, austere and fierce.* Further down the hall she glances at another similar-styled picture of a ballerina. *And look at you, so calm and sure and brave.* She walks back down the creaky floorboards to the first picture and then back to the second. And then once again. *Is that the same woman? Is it supposed to be?* She stands looking first at the praying woman with her veil and clasped hands. *I know you, bitch.* Then again studying the ballerina in her loose shawl and dancing shoes, with an expression, light and serene, Simone smiles. *I know you too. Not so well yet, but I will.* She taps the glass and moves on.

Passing Jasper's room Simone feels compelled to rap on his door to say goodnight. He answers red-eyed.

"What's wrong, Jasper?"

"I've just been dumped."

"What? Why? How?"

Jasper beckons Simone in, and she closes the door

behind her. "Just been FaceTiming Flo, who announced four pieces of news." He stands by his bed, arms folded. "One, her mum died last night unexpectedly. Two, she woke this morning convinced she should now have kids of her own. Three, if I'm prepared to move to Ullapool and become a father, she'll have them with me. And four, If I'm not then she needs to move on."

"Wow. And?"

"And I'm not, so she is."

Simone barges past Jasper and grabs his coat off the bed. "Come on."

"Where to?"

"The pub."

Abandoning the idea of an early night Simone marches a silent Jasper up the dark lane, under the shadowy alders and hazels to the Inn. She deposits him in a quiet corner. "Wainwrights?"

"Please." Jasper replies. "And possibly a teeny whiskey."

Simone returns with three glasses which she balances on the flat parts of an unevenly hewn tabletop. "How are you doing?"

"I'm OK." Jasper takes two of the three glasses. "It's all just a bit of a shock. First, her mum. Her sudden decision to have kids. Then the fact she was willing to have them with me. As you know, it's been a bit of a long-distance, part-time relationship, so that was a shocker."

"I remember you telling me about her back in the coffee shop. Flo with the mad red hair and a satellite dish the size of a shed." Simone looks at him over her G & T, wondering quite how to manage this. "You ... er ... don't fancy kids then?"

"Maybe. In a few years or so, but I'm not ready

yet. I wanted to travel a bit before settling down into all that. I never did the gap-year thing, so hoped to see a bit of the world first."

Simone tilts her head questioningly.

"Africa maybe, or South America, or Asia. Somewhere exotic. Not Europe or North America, too samey. Somewhere proper foreign where things want to bite and sting you all the time." Jasper takes a sip of his not so teeny whiskey. "Some exotic-sounding place where you have absolutely no idea how or why they live as they do."

"Like where?" Simone asks.

"Dunno. But the list is endless, isn't it? Namibia, Burundi, Botswana, and that's just Africa. Or how about Java or Sumatra or somewhere down there. Anywhere that's not like anywhere else. Somewhere where you can plant your feet in the red earth, breathe in the warm air and think – I may never be here again, but I was once in this place." Jasper slumps back against the wall and again folds his arms. "I remember a quote by the management writer Charles Handy. He said the point of travel is to audition new gods. See 'new things and things anew'. Something like that."

"Interesting idea," Simone says. "How long have you fancied wandering the world auditioning new gods then?"

"Since I was about ten, I suppose. When I first fancied that glamorous career as a long-distance lorry driver."

"What stopped you?" Simone asks. "Wandering the world that is, not being a ten-year-old truck driver."

Jasper fiddles with the hardened red wax of an unlit candle. "Usual lame, half-witted reasons as everyone else, I guess: mortgage, career, fear."

"Fear of what?"

"Don't know exactly. Fear of not liking it and coming straight back, maybe. Fear of liking it too much and never coming back. Fear of losing momentum in my career, such as it is. Fear of being incessantly bitten and stung. The list is as long as the countries to be scared in."

Simone's attention briefly shifts to Jasper's pint glass with the word *Wainwrights* engraved diagonally up the side. "I really must Google that bloke," she mutters.

Jasper changes the subject. "And what do you make of our very own Dr Wainwright?"

"Al? I think I'd rather fancy him if I were twenty years older, or him younger. He's got something of an old Al Pacino about him. I wonder what Al stands for?"

"Alan."

"Alan, seriously?"

"Yeah, I asked him."

Oh dear, that's disappointing. Alan Pacino? No, that doesn't work at all. Simone looks over Jasper's head at an assortment of old climbing gear nailed to the wall.

Jasper turns around to see what has caught Simone's eye, to be confronted by the riveted soles of hobnailed boots dangling inches above his head. "Did people actually climb in this stuff?" He studies the boots, crampons and rucksacks for a moment, then turns back to Simone. "And, how about you? Kids on the agenda at some point?"

"Probably, at some point," she says. "But like you, not for a few years, despite the ticking clock."

"I tell you what." Jasper clicks a finger and thumb. "We can make a pact. If we're still both sad and single in a decade's time we can get back in touch, hook up and have our own family."

"Hmm ... that's a gracious offer," Simone says. "But you'll have to let me think about it. Say, for about a decade or so, just to make sure it's not a rebound proposal." She pulls gently on his cuff. "Is there no other way of navigating your predicament with Flo? Could she move down to yours, maybe?"

Jasper takes a sip of whiskey and shakes his head once left and right. "No chance. She's Scottish born and bred. Her family is there, and her home is there. Most of all, her heart is there. And how can you ask anyone to move their heart from where it belongs?"

Simone puts her hand over her mouth. "That's sweet. You're not always the arse you make out, are you Oran?"

"Well, I'm enough of an arse that I won't move to Scotland and become a father."

"You're quite the opposite for that, in my opinion."

"Really?" Jasper asks. "How so?"

"Seriously? Has your own family history taught you nothing? If your heart wasn't in it, it would have got messy at some point, wouldn't it? Just a matter of time. So, those little baby Florences will be mighty glad when they end up with a dad who's fully on board, rather than one whose own heart is still wandering the plains of Patagonia or the jungles of Java. Trust me on this one, Jasper. A woman knows."

Jasper takes another sip and looks Simone dead in the eye. "Yeah. Fair point."

SIMONE AND JASPER are taking an evening stroll along the river to Eden Water, a modest but rudely picturesque lake. Scots pine and spruce roll along the lower shores before raising up its northern slopes to make a grand green amphitheater a hundred metres high. The last of the sun glances off the high wooded hilltop while down below mist forms on Edendale's inky waters.

Despite the view, Simone is walking along with hands in pockets and chin on chest. "Tell me, Jasper."

Jasper is transfixed by the impeccably mirrored sunset in the lake. "Yeah?"

"We've talked about the shifts occurring in me, but what about you? Is any of this impacting you much?"

"God yes, of course." His eyes don't move from the dual sunset. "I can't say I have an alter-ego like your Miss Andersen to battle and bury, but I am learning that there might be a place for all the fanciful philosophy that loiters in the back of my brain." *Secretly lurking while I get on with the deadening monotony of everyday life.*

They stop at the lakeshore and Jasper points silently at fish breaking the surface to gorge on the mist of mayflies and midges living inches above.

"I used to think I was weird, y'know? Folk around me always seemed happy enough, busying themselves with everyday mundanity. I didn't get it. No one seemed to care about the big stuff,"

"Big stuff?" Simone pulls up her hood against the descending cold.

"Yeah, like the stuff our existential coach got us to focus on. Life and living and the point of it all, and indeed what it means if it all means nothing at all. Now there's a trip." Jasper stops to lean against an enormous boulder that fell from the rock face above a thousand years ago. He looks up, trying to identify the hole and imagine the spectacle.

Simone leans on the boulder facing him. "There's an awful lot about meaning in there."

"There is, but then there's a lot about meaning everywhere. It's at the core of everything when you think about it, Simm. Religion, cults, gangs, work, career, family, community, it's endless. And I think it might be at the core of a lot of our coaching to come, even if the coachees aren't aware of it." Jasper tuts. "Or maybe it's just me. I search for meaning in everything and it drives me nuts, to be honest. Oh, just to live life on the shiny surface, eh?" *The shiny effortless surface.*

They stumble along the rubble path in single file.

"Ever heard of Viktor Frankl?" Jasper asks over his shoulder.

"Can't say I have." Simone replies.

"Now, that's a read. This Austrian psychiatrist survived Auschwitz and he believed that finding meaning in his suffering kept his spirit alive and gave him a reason to go on each day. He said it was his search for some scrap of meaning, among all that death and depravity, that stopped him simply surrendering to it all. He says he could tell when his comrades had begun their final descent. They would smoke their last cigarette in the evening and by morning they were gone." He glances behind to make sure he is not talking to himself. "Imagine not just surviving all that nihilism but trying to make sense of it."

"That's heavy stuff for an evening stroll," Simone kicks the back of Jasper's walking boot.

"I know, I'm sorry. I bet most tourists don't come here and bother themselves with this shit. Bloody meaning-making-monkey-mind at it again."

"Monkey what?" Simone shouts as they pass a

plunging waterfall.

"Monkey mind – that's what the Buddhists call it when you can't stop your brain turning over." Jasper pats the top of his head. "Imagine though. The power of meaning, enough to keep yourself alive, metaphorically, and in Frankl's case, literally. After the war he even developed his own form of therapy based around it. Logotherapy – *meaning therapy*. What a gig, eh?"

They stop to make friends with some friendly Herwickes and watch the skittish lambs play king-of-the-castle on an upturned water barrel.

"I always thought I was a bit of a freak to be honest. I seemed to be the only person I knew who troubled themselves with this stuff. I'd try to talk to friends and girlfriends about it but always got short thrift. 'That's interesting' was about the best I'd get. Makes you feel quite alien, y'know?"

Simone puts a sympathetic arm around his shoulder. "Poor monkey."

"Then *boom!*" He claps his hands together. "We hook up with those coaches in London. And not only do I discover other people actually do think that way, but they even make a living from it. Now that *is* a gig."

The remnants of day fade and they head for the rickety river bridge. Midway over the planks they stop to watch the shallow river thrash below on its way out to the sea.

"Would you fancy it?" Simone asks.

"Fancy what?"

"Coaching, as a job?"

"What?" Jasper says. "Make a living from having deep and meaningful conversations that help others? Now, that is what I think Aristotle himself might have called eudaemonia – a good life."

"And a life well-lived," Simone says.

They step from the footbridge and walk back along the lane in near darkness. Strolling in the easy silence that has found its way naturally into how they are together. They walk straight past the fat friar and decide to fend for themselves again tonight.

"Pizza or pasta?" Simone asks as they scrunch up the driveway.

"What the hell." Jasper picks up speed along the gravel. "Let's have *both*!"

FOR THE LAST lunchtime Jasper joins Simone on a stone bench by the ivy-clad back wall. He shoves a pile of unread newspapers along the bench.

"Afternoon. So, what's your final verdict on Mr and Mrs Al then?" he asks.

Simone is facing the sun, eyes closed, and murmurs, "They're good, really good,"

"C'mon Simm, you know the drill – *good* is not a word."

"True." She takes a moment. "Well, you've got teachers and trainers … and then you've got these guys. I'm not even sure what to call them. Are they group coaches? Group leaders? Facilitators? Tutors?"

"I know exactly what you mean. They seem to move in and out of those roles all the time, along with teaching us the technical stuff." Jasper points at a small muntjac beside a rhododendron.

"Sweet," Simone whispers. "I once read about tiny dik-dik antelopes in East Africa, only about a foot tall. When there's a lion around, they follow it, so they know where it is all the time. So, you have this bizarre scene of a tiny antelope stalking a lion."

"*National Geographic* by any chance?" Jasper asks.

"Of course. That's my way of vicariously wandering the world, Jasper." She pats the pile of papers and supplements on the bench between them. "Two hours every month, no jabs required."

"We've spooked the dik-dik. Look, there it goes. Anyway, back to Al and Alison?"

"The way they can just sit there with the group is extraordinary. They clearly feel no need to lecture us or demonstrate their knowledge for the sake of it. They're able to sit quietly while the group just reflects and processes. Alison said to us all it was something about 'holding' the group or 'containing' it, or something."

"New one on me," Jasper says.

"They seem to contribute only what's needed and when, helping to create those static-free channels we talked about the other day. We said good coaches do that in one-to-one scenarios, but these guys are doing it with the entire group. Amazing." Simone closes her eyes again. "Silence is a powerful thing, don't you think?"

Sensing a bear trap, Jasper just smiles and nods, silently.

"Seems to me it goes hand in hand with the other skills of questioning and listening." Simone juts out her thumb for emphasis. "One. You ask good questions, then you're silent. "Two—" She flicks up a forefinger. "—you listen to the answers and stay silent." Up goes the index finger. "Then three. Based only on what you've heard, and not your own mental flights of fancy, you make your next move. Seriously. How such a simple thing can take so much discipline is flabbergasting, and the power of it equally astonishing. And yet we're generally so terrible at it."

"Sorry, I tuned out minutes ago.

"Funny. And it doesn't end there. There are all these different silences too and there's a real skill in knowing which sort you're dealing with."

"Different sorts of silence?" Jasper repeats.

"I'd not really thought about it before, but when you focus, you can tune into all the different types of quiet."

"Like?"

"Like ... silence when someone is just reacting. Or silence when someone is processing a thought. Silence when someone is trying to make sense of a feeling. Silence when someone needs time or air or space. Maybe a recovery silence when someone needs to take stock of what they've just learnt or experienced. Or a silence when they need stillness just to commune with themselves."

"That's a lot of silences," Jasper says.

"And they're all useful because they're all working silences. Does that make sense?"

"Absolutely."

"Then of course there are the vacuous silences. The silences where someone has left the conversation. They're thinking about their to-do list or dinner plans or whatever. They're very different silences and I think maybe I can spot them better now."

"Fascinating," Jasper says quietly.

Simone looks over, stony-faced.

"No, I mean it. It makes total sense." Jasper shifts himself on the bench to face her. "Think about all of our interminable meetings back in the office. Some of those can be full of long silences, but you always have some intangible sense of what they might mean. It might be a pregnant pause, with something useful to follow. Or a barren, tumbleweed pause, where nobody's really got a clue what's going on. Or one of those excruciating pauses where there might be silence in the room but the space above everyone's head is teeming with thought bubbles, seldom saying anything constructive."

They share a knowing grunt and lean back against the cool ivy wall.

Jasper's thoughts return to Latte Central in London and how he and Simone have grown from casual acquaintances to friends and now something more. *We jest and tease, sure, but when it comes to this coaching, what it might mean and where it might lead, we are solidly on the same page.* His mind wanders as he absorbs the still and quiet of the valley. *This whole space feels like some sort of transitional experience, leading to something or somewhere new. I wonder…*

"Last day tomorrow," Simone suddenly announces. "Do you know what you're doing?"

Jasper blinks back into the sunlight. "A bit more theory I think and some more practice and then that's it … all done. Shame really."

"We can have a full debrief on the way back down the motorway, can't we, after we've climbed this mountain of yours."

"By the way," Simone says. "Guess what I discovered from Alison earlier."

"Go on."

"I think you'll like this."

"Go on."

"Turns out they run an advanced group-coaching programme down south."

Jasper swings around, his descending spirits immediately lifted. "You're shitting me?"

Eyes still closed, Simone smiles and pats him on

the thigh. "No, Jasper, I am most definitely not shitting you."

Jasper composes himself. He lets a strange, serene moment pass, then unable to contain himself elbows Simone in the side. "Are we up for it?"

"Oh yes," they say in unison, grinning at the sun like a couple of baking lizards.

SUN POURS IN through the enormous sash windows and bounces off the chipped and discoloured Butler sink. *Maybe eight hundred metres isn't so bad. Hardly Everest, is it?* Simone thinks as she conducts the rucksack audit on the kitchen table. "Water – check. Fruit – check," she announces. "Tinfoil blanket – check. Packed lunch – check. Water – check."

"You did water twice," Jasper contributes from a dusty armchair next to the AGA.

"Both the Als say you can't have enough, particularly in summer." Simone continues. "Torch – check. Battery pack – check. Mint cake for up the top – check."

"And who's going to carry that little lot up?" Al asks as he strolls into the kitchen with an empty coffee mug. "Are you going to be the gentleman, Jasper, or let Simone lug it up?" He flashes his smile.

Simone looks over at Jasper. "I'm all for equal rights, buuuuuut…"

"Seriously, guys, what hills have you climbed before?" Al asks.

"I did Coombe Hill once," Jasper says quietly into his tea mug.

"I once went up Leith Hill," Simone adds, even more self-consciously into the rucksack.

"I don't know where either of those places are, so I'm guessing they're not eight hundred meters?"

Jasper and Simone shrug.

"Look, I'm not saying you can't do it and I'm not saying you can't enjoy it. But I am saying get your skates on, because it'll take you eight hours up and down, assuming you don't get lost. By the same token, take your time, stay on the path and then the chimney and you should be fine. Prepare to be completely buggered when you get back down though. I wouldn't arrange any last night parties at the Inn. And finally, be prepared for instant weather changes. What you've got now is no guarantee of what you'll have in an hour." Al wanders back out the kitchen with his fresh mug of coffee. "Other than that – enjoy."

"He's being a tad melodramatic, isn't he?" Jasper says.

"Are you sure about that?" Simone nods towards the window.

"Great, pissing down already." Jasper loads the rucksack onto his back. "Fair enough, let's go."

They set off in waterproofs and hoods, walking towards the foot of the hill where the ascent begins. A walk-in to the start of a climb in Scotland could be a punishing ordeal itself, but in chocolate-box Cumbria it is a typically more civilised affair, passing campsites, farms and on this occasion a dilapidated red telephone box.

They stop for a moment at the phone box and look up at the path, following it right, left, right, left before it disappears ominously around a blind cliff face.

"You still up for it?" Jasper asks, grappling with the rucksack straps.

"We've got the mountain gods to guide us and the map-app as backup, what could possibly go wrong?"

Simone replies, full of non-existent bravado.

"Jeezuz, Sim, don't say that. Look above you, any-bloody-thing could go wrong."

Simone feels the need for some calming logic. "Look, you've done the Chilterns' highest hill and I've done the best Surrey has to offer. I checked, and together that's nearly two thirds of the way up this hill. So, between us we've nearly done it already."

"I'm not entirely sure that's how it works, you know."

Sensing fermenting panic, Simone tries to take early control. "Don't be such a wuss, let's go."

They walk for another hour up through forest paths following the smell of pines and moss until they emerge above the tree line where the trees give way to scrub and heather.

This feels more like a mountain. Simone stops. "How are you doing, Jasper?"

"Worryingly knackered already, but still determined. You?"

"Feeling blissfully ignorant of what to expect, so it's just one step at a time, onwards and upwards."

For another hour they trudge a muddy, steep path up the side of a ghyll, freezing water crashing down from one waterfall to the next. They take a breather on a damp grass bank next to one of the marble green pools.

"This is lovely. Shall we call it a day here?" Simone suggests. "Only joking." *Well, half joking.*

"Onwards and upwards, those were your very words." Jasper passes her the water bottle. "See those big craggy lumps up there?" He points towards a clearing sky. "We've just got to crawl in between them, then climb straight up through and we'll be out onto the top. Then it's a saunter back down round the side and follow the gorge to the road and back."

Simone feels a sudden jolt to the system. "Excuse me, did you say crawl?"

"Maybe not crawl then. Scramble."

She feels a gnarling onset of panic. "I'm really not liking either of those words, Mr Oran! I didn't come up here to effing crawl or scramble around anything. I came up here for a walk, Jasper. A bloody walk!"

"And we will be walking ... for the most part. Al showed me the chimney pics in his guidebook yesterday, it's not that bad. You can't fall far because each boulder sits just above the next. Just like messing about on a giant climbing frame. What's not to like?"

"You're sounding far too nonchalant about this, Jasper. Are you trying to convince me or you? Here's the deal." Simone takes a gulp of air. "I'll come with you as far as the beginning of that stupid chimney thing. Then we have a sandwich, and we reassess. But no promises – OK?"

"Okey-doke."

I'm serious. I have absolutely no compunction about walking straight back down the way we came up if I don't like the look of it."

"Okey-dokey," Jasper says again, throwing the rucksack back on.

After another uncomfortable hour stepping sideways up along the scree of the lower slopes, they arrive at the bottom of the semi-enclosed gully called The Chimney.

"Well, that's not scary-looking at all," Simone says, feeling sick.

"Al says it's called The Chimney because of its appearance obviously, but also because everyone who goes in through the bottom always comes back out at the top."

"Really? Is that true?" Simone sits dejectedly on a small flat rock.

"Allegedly." Jasper points towards the entrance. "It looks scary but apparently when you get into it, it's just not. From the outside it looks like Middle Earth stuff but from inside its just knee-high boulders running straight to the top like an escalator."

"You're so full of shit," Simone says, feeling incredibly weary. "You know as little as me about this place."

"Well, you make a fair point, although, I did sit up in bed all last night reading up on the route and checking out comments and images online."

"Really?" Simone feels a tiny wave of relief.

"Cross my heart."

"Honestly?"

"Swear to God. I'll level with you, Simm. There's one slightly dodgy step that takes a bit of nerve apparently. But that's right at the entrance."

She looks over, confused. "Is it easy or not?"

"Once you're over that, it's just one foot in front of the other, all the way to the top. Scout's honour." Jasper raises a three-fingered salute.

"One dodgy step?"

"Just the one. Even that's supposed to be a bit of fun if you're willing to slide down it on your backside. Which you have to in the snow apparently. You pick your way up one side of the boulder, which is made easy because of all the ice-axe and crampon scars on there. Clamber up onto the top and slide down the other side. And if you want to bail out, you just do the same in reverse."

Simone feels another small layer of anxiety lift.

"Then it's just a thigh-pumping, knee-crunching boulder stairway for a couple of hundred metres and we're out on top. That leaves a jaunty hands-in-pockets skip across to the summit and we're done."

Simone knows it is now or never for her. "OK, let's go. Now!"

Ninety minutes later they stumble to the rocky summit cairn.

"That was without doubt the hardest and scariest thing I have ever done," Simone pants.

Jasper can hardly breath. "Oh yes."

They pace about the summit, gathering themselves and their breath, eventually coming to a standstill, then collapsing down onto the rocks at the foot of the cairn.

"Well," Jasper says still breathing heavily, "are we going to give Miss Andersen her sky burial after all that?"

"Already done," Simone says, still taking in large gulps of air. "What? Really?"

"Yes. I made my peace and said my goodbyes and left her at the bottom of that fucking chimney. If I was going to die in there, I didn't want to do it with her still on my back. I figure the wind and the birds will still find her down there, and I get to emerge at the summit a new woman.

Jasper smiles and squeezes her knee. "Ready to see new things and things anew, eh?"

Simone leans back against the cairn, feeling battered, bruised and relieved. She looks out onto a view of distant mountains she's never seen before, feeling oddly nostalgic. *Thank you, Miss Andersen. Thank you, and goodbye.* She lets out a large puff of air. "Now that's done Jasp, I'm ready to celebrate."

"Oh yeah, how's that?" he says, wearily.

"You know this Cumbrian ale you've been enjoying by the gallon? I think I'm ready for my first pint of it." She slaps Jasper's knee, hauls herself to her feet and heads towards the path down.

"Come on," she shouts over her shoulder. "Wainwright's waiting!"

THE JOURNEY BACK south takes an age. The winner of the motorway coin toss was the M6 and so Simone and Jasper are stationary somewhere between Manchester and Birmingham.

"This is painful," Simone groans, enunciating every word with her forehead on the steering wheel. "Why-won't-this-bloody-traffic-move?" she moans. "What-the-hell-is-a-smart-motorway-anyway?"

Engines are off and people are getting out to stretch their legs, smoke cigarettes and visit the hard shoulder to address other personal needs. Jasper and Simone have completed their weeks debrief and exhausted every lame childhood car-game they can think of, so Jasper flicks on the radio, just in time to hear an emergency announcement by the prime minister.

"Good evening. The coronavirus is the biggest threat this country has faced for decades. All over the world, we are seeing the devastating impact of this invisible killer. Therefore, from this evening I must give the British people a very simple instruction – you must stay at home."

Simone looks across at Jasper. "Oh my God!"

Jasper frowns back. "What the bloody fuck?"

Chapter Three
COACHING, LIFE AND LOCKDOWN

"YOU DON'T LOOK well, Simm." Jasper tilts his screen forward. *Not well at all.*

"Don't feel it." Simone slumps back in her swivel chair.

"What's wrong?"

"I'm struggling."

Jasper pushes his face up to the camera. "With?"

"Everything." She ignores the brown Burmese that jumps onto her lap. "It's nearly nine months since we came back from the Lakes, Jasper. If I'd had any inkling that would have been our last taste of freedom, I'd…" Simone plants a palm on her forehead.

"You'd what?"

"I don't know." She thuds her forehead into the butt of her palm. "Enjoyed it more. Been more present. I don't know. Found a cave to live in, maybe." She lifts Snowflake onto the floor. "Go away, cat."

Jaspers peers down the screen. *This ain't like Simone. She adores that moggy.* "You'd have been no better off though, would you? A cave up there or one down here. What would be the difference?"

Simone looks forlorn down the camera. "I don't know. The view, maybe?"

"Eh?"

"All I can see from my balcony is an empty parade of crappy shops."

"Show me."

Simone takes her laptop to the window and points the camera out over the balcony. "That's what Snowflake and I sit and look at every night. A dark, empty parade of shops. With a tin of tuna for her and a glass of wine for me. That's our life, Jasper. Day in, night out." She stares for a moment at a fox crossing the deserted parade. "Anyway, enough of my mithering. How's North West Seven, you jammy bugger?"

"Yeah, I know. Lady Luck came good for me on this."

"Go on, torture me. What can you see out of your fancy heath side apartment then?"

Jasper awkwardly nods at one window, then another. "The city lights from that window, and a bit of the heath from that one."

Simone drops her head in her palm again.

Jasper winces. "I know, I'm sorry. I shouldn't have got this place, really. It was sheer luck time wise. But if Lady Luck was putting out..."

Simone looks up resting her chin on her fist, saying nothing.

"Look," Jasper says. "Boris says that in two weeks we can have some limited contact and meet in bubbles for outdoor exercise. Why don't we form a bubble and you come here? I can stuff some healthy pasties and Pinot in a rucky and we can wander over to the heath for some supposed exercise. Get you some air and some views. What do you think?"

Simone drags her hand down her chin to her neck and manages a small smile. "That would be amazing."

"Great. Then two weeks Saturday, get the Tube to Hampstead for about eleven o'clock and I'll meet you outside the station. We can grab a coffee and then wander onto the heath for the afternoon."

"Sounds fabulous."

They both wave at the screen.

... *Click* ...

"SO, WHAT DO you think?" Simone's cochee looks sternly through the screen.

"Well, it sounds good to me," Simone answers.

"So, you think I should go for it?"

Simone hesitates. "I think so." *Why is she being weird? Is she testing me?*

"OK, well, thanks for your time. I think this will be the last session, though. I'll contact HR and let them know. Goodbye, Simone."

... *Click* ...

Simone stares at the black screen. *But ... I was ... I didn't...* She jumps as the phone on her desk chimes FaceTime.

"Simone, hi."

"Oh, hi." She tries to focus on Jasper's flickering image.

"You OK?" he asks.

"I think so."

"You don't sound it. What's up?"

Simone screws up her face, embarrassed. "I think I just lost my first coachee."

"Hah!" Jasper blurts out. "Oops, sorry, wasn't expecting that. What happened?"

Simone props the phone against her cheap plastic desk lamp. "We've been talking about a potential career move for her out of the company and this week it came to a head."

"And?"

"And—" Simone starts. "—after we'd talked through all the pros and cons and risks, etcetera, it looked like she'd reached a decision this week to go for it."

"So, what's the problem?"

Simone scans back through their previous six sessions together. "I'm not sure. After having listened to her talk herself into it, I agreed with her conclusion and said I thought she should go for it too."

"Ah."

"Ah? Ah what?" *What does bloody ah mean?*

Jasper fiddles with his phone to get it at the right angle and brings it to rest against his coffee mug.

"Ah, what?" Simone repeats, desperate to hear the answers that the *Ah* promises.

"I think … I mean … I wonder…"

"Oh please, spit it out."

"Well, I wonder if you might have been talking to yourself."

"What are you talking about, Jasper? I was talking to her."

"Well, yes. But it doesn't sound like you were coaching her, not in the end at least. It sounds like you were maybe colluding and cheerleading her a bit."

Simone sighs. "Forgive me, Jasper, but we did all our coach training together, and I don't recall either of us learning anything about cheerleading."

"What I mean is, I wonder if you were subconsciously egging her on to make the leap."

"Why on earth would I do that?"

"Because it's what you want to do, isn't it? You've been talking about changing jobs since we came back from the Lakes. Since before we went up there, in fact."

"So?"

"Sooo, maybe your conversation wasn't so much with her as with yourself."

Simone slumps back in her chair and stares at the keyboard, silent.

Jasper waits for a few seconds and then taps the screen. "You still there? You've frozen. Simone?"

"Still here," she whispers.

"Oh, OK." Jasper waits another few seconds. "Does that chime at all?"

"Yes, of course it does." *What a bloody idiot.*

"Let me get off this tiddly screen and I'll Zoom you. Give us a minute."

Simone sits meditatively, her arm flopped down the side of the chair stroking Snowflake's chin. *Your mum's a bloody idiot, Snowy.* A moment later, she clicks on the link and Jasper looms large on her flat screen.

"You've had your hair cut," she says.

"Yep."

"How did you manage that in lockdown?"

"I was sick of my lockdown locks, so I ordered some clippers and got to it." Jasper swivels his head to reveal close cropped back and sides.

"Not bad actually," Simone says.

"Yeah, also lost some of the grey creeping through at the temples at the same time. Job done."

"My, my, Mr Oran, such vanity."

"Not so vain I won't take a pair of clippers to my own head though."

"True. Anyway, talk to me about my rookie error. I can't believe, after all we've learnt, I fell into the trap of actually encouraging a coachee to take a particular course of action." Simone taps her temple with her pencil, then sticks it behind her ear. "What an idiot."

"I wouldn't be too hard on yourself, Simm. It might seem like basic coaching stuff, but it's still one of the hardest things to stop yourself doing, apparently."

"Really," Simone says, hopefully.

"Yeah, especially if there's some transference going on. It can play havoc with the interaction between coach and coachee, so I've been reading."

"Whoa, what? Transference? What's that you've been pouring into your little brain during lockdown, then?"

Jasper leans out of sight for a moment and returns to view, waving a black and white paperback. Simone tries to focus on the blurred cover. "Sit still a minute." She squints while the grizzled cover portrait comes to a stop. "Freud?" she squawks. "What's he got to do with anything this century?"

Jasper smiles and taps the cover. "I'm finding quite a bit of use in here, actually."

"Really, about coaching?"

"Sure. Particularly this transference and counter-transference stuff."

"Go on then." Simone leans back in her swivel chair and folds her arms. "Educate me."

"OK." Jasper puts the book aside. "According to our pal Sigmund, when a psychoanalyst works at depth with a client, the relationship becomes so important that the client eventually starts to project onto the therapist, thoughts and feelings they have had about other significant people in their lives." Jasper peers into the screen. "Have you frozen again or are you bored already?"

"You've still got me. Go on."

"This transfer of feelings from a different time, place and person is called transference and can lead the client to have both good and bad feeling towards the therapist that are actually remnants from previous key relationships – anger, suspicion, envy, affection, even love."

"Really," Simone says, flatly. *And ludicrous sexual thoughts, knowing Freud.*

"Apparently, Freud first caught on to this when his clients seemed to regularly fall in love with him. Though to be fair, his client base was exclusively young Victorian women. Go figure."

Simone raises an eyebrow. *And there it is, ladies and gentlemen.*

"Anyway, that aside, he found that examining the transferred feelings and working them through really helped clients understand themselves and their relationships better. It's probably worth noting that Freud never acted on any of these projected affections, allegedly. That would've just stirred up a whole Viennese hornets' nest, wouldn't it?"

Simone shrugs. "And my coachee debacle this morning?"

"Well, that's where the counter-transference comes in. That is, the feelings and reactions of the therapist, or in this case coach, triggered by working with particular clients and issues."

"How? I don't have any powerful feelings for this coachee one way or another. I don't get it," Simone pleads.

"No, but you do for their situation, don't you?"

Simone unfolds her arms and straightens up. "Hang on." She points her index finger at the screen. "Are we saying that because I'm thinking about a career change, that when I'm working with someone facing the same dilemma or opportunity, I unconsciously encourage them to do what I would want to do?"

Jasper nods. "We are."

"Well, I never." Simone removes the pencil from behind her ear and taps it on her notebook. *Obvious really.* "OK, I can buy that." She slaps her pencil down. "I'll give you and the weird Victorian shrink that one."

"I'm sure Herr Sigmund would be thrilled." Jasper smiles. "Anyway, now I've moved up to NW7 I'm on the doorstep of the Freud Museum so when you come visit, we could wander down there and have a poke round if you fancied it."

"I've said it before, Jasper, and I'll say it again – you spoil me."

"I know. Any developments on the job front?"

"None really."

"Nothing?"

"Nope. Remember that *stages-of-change* model that Alison taught us up in the Lakes?"

"I do."

"I think I'm well and truly stuck at the *contemplation* stage."

"I thought you were keen to move on, particularly if they keep insisting on promoting you?" Jasper tuts.

"I know. The irony is not lost on me. But I just don't want to move up into the senior echelons. I'd be bored crapless."

"I see the potty mouth is coming on nicely."

"Well, that's lockdown for you. God, I miss my team. I see most of them every week, but we just don't have the fun and energy we had in the office. Everyone seems so apathetic and distant. I can't blame them, I feel like that myself, but I just don't have the energy to gee them up all the time. I love them dearly, but I've barely got enough energy to get myself through each week, working at the same desk staring at the same screen."

Jasper nods agreement. "Remind me, what's the next stage after *contemplation*?"

"*Preparation.*"

"Right. So, you need to actually make a decision before you move on to that stage?"

"Exactly. Though the pandemic has put all recruitment and promotion on hold for now, so I've got a bit of a stay of execution."

"More time to ruminate, then," Jasper says.

"Indeed. Anyway, gotta go. I've got a new coachee at twelve."

"Oh great. Let me know how you get on."

"Will do." Simone rolls the mouse across her desk and waves.

... *Click* ...

"HI, SEAN, NICE to meet you. How would you like to use your time today?"

"I'm not sure, to be honest."

Simone tenses. *Oh crap!* "OK, no problem. Let's talk about how things are with you currently. What are the main things taking up your time and energy at the moment, that sort of thing?" *What if he's got nothing? What do we talk about if he doesn't know what to talk about? Crap! Why do people come to coaching if they have nothing to talk about?*

Sean's face remains expressionless as he peers into the screen from his blurred backdrop.

Trust the process, trust the process. People always have something on their mind they want to talk about if they feel able. "You seem unsure where to start, Sean." Simone studies his expression frantically to gauge her new coachee's mood. *He seems a bit stressed to me. No, nervous or impatient maybe. Or irritated. Oh, I don't know.* "What do you think brings you to coaching? Do you have any sense at this stage what you'd like to get from it?" *OK, that's enough now. Give him some space.*

"Well, I appreciate your time, and I don't want to waste it. I just don't know if my stuff is coaching worthy, really."

Stuff – that's a start. "Well, the purpose of these sessions is exactly that, Sean. It's to talk about what's on your mind and see where it leads and decide if it's going to be of any benefit to you talking it through with me."

"Right," Sean says, stone-faced.

"And where it leads can often be somewhere very different to where you initially think it might."

"Right." A relieved smile suddenly appears on Sean's face.

"So, what's on your mind, Sean? Start anywhere you like." *Phew!*

Simone's new coachee shifts, trying to get comfortable in his chair. He takes a breath but keeps it in, hesitating. He winces slightly, tipping his head left and right, seeming to weigh up his opening comments. Eventually, his breath comes out, and he starts. "Surprise, surprise, my main issue at the moment seems to be homeworking."

"OK, what is it about home working that you'd like to discuss?"

"Where to start. I'm struggling with my workload and my time management. I'm getting increasingly impatient with my team. I'm feeling dislocated from the job and worrying about the longer-term career prospects of being cut off from the office. And that's just the stuff that comes immediately to mind."

"Well, there's certainly a lot in there to unpack."

"Yeah, sorry."

"Don't be. That's the whole point of these discussions. To find out what's going on for you on the inside and get it outside so we can explore it."

"Is it?"

"It is." Simone smiles reassuringly. "That alone will give some clarity about what's going on with you. We can examine it together, explore connections, understand cause and effect, categorise issues, prioritise actions, that sort of thing."

"OK." Sean flumps back into his chair, appearing relieved.

"Then, if you think it could be helpful, we can work on developing some plans or strategies on how best to move forward and improve these various issues for you." Simone starts to relax and remember her training. *Create and contain the right conditions so they can open up and work with you. Calming reassurance that we can work this stuff out – that's the ticket. Hold the energy, hold the space.*

"That sounds encouraging, but where to begin?" Sean hunches his shoulders.

"We can begin by deciding where to begin."

"Come again?"

"If you had to prioritise all of those home-working issues you just listed, which one feels the heaviest to you?"

"The heaviest?"

"Yes. By that, I mean which feels like it's taking the most energy from you? Sitting most heavily on your shoulders? We'll get to them all, but which seems like the most important place to start? Top of the list."

"That's easy," Sean says, rolling up his sleeves and moving closer to his screen.

"And then he says ... 'none of those things'."

"None of them?" Jasper says, peering through the screen.

"Nope."

"So, what was his priority?"

"Building a garden shed!" Simone grins as she takes a sip of green tea.

"What?" Jasper laughs.

"Building a garden shed."

"What the hell's that got to do with anything?"

"According to the coachee, whose name shall, of course, remain confidential, everything."

"Everything?" Jasper repeats back.

"Yes. Turns out most of his issues stem from not having a decent, quiet space to work in at home. He's got kids running wild while they're supposed to be home schooling, and he's working from one cramped corner in his kitchen-diner while his wife tries to work in the other."

"Welcome to 2021." Jasper swigs from his metallic water bottle.

"We discussed it for two hours straight, and everything tied back to his increased stress levels from having no proper space to work in."

"So, he wants you to help him build a shed?"

"Hardly, though I have become pretty handy at DIY during lockdown. He wants me to help him sort out and prioritise his time and task management and keep him accountable to it, keep his feet to the fire, as he puts it. That way he can create and ring-fence clear downtime and build his shed."

"Interesting coaching gig that, Simm – shedding."

"Shed is a bit of an understatement though. He's a structural engineer and it sounds like quite a sizable project. He lives on the edge of a village with a large piece of land, so it's going to be two storeys with heating, plumbing, electrics. Sounds like he's planning a satellite office out there."

"And how do you think you'll find working with him?"

"I'm a bit ambivalent, actually."

"Yeah?"

"Once we worked out how everything is connected to this one major issue, he put his project manager hat straight on and started figuring out time schedules and milestones and all that. So, in one respect, a lot of the main work has been done and now it's just a case of keeping him to plan."

"But?"

"The other thing is that he's a real Type A character. He seems to get wound up about everything and by his own admission, that's taking a toll."

"In what way?"

"Struggling to sleep, getting snappy at home, drinking too much in the evening. He even says he's getting paranoid about his team not doing their work properly and about what his own manager is thinking about him and the work he's doing."

"Sounds quite a meaty assignment then."

"It does. But that whiff of stress-related stuff is making me twitchy. What if it veers towards mental health issues? What do we do then? They didn't cover in our training what we do when coaching approaches counselling, did they?"

"I've been idly wondering about that myself. It seems a lot of folks are struggling with this home-working, in one way or another. And I'm finding most of the material people bring in is compounded with home-working issues."

Simone feels a knot winding up in her stomach.

"We've come to this at quite an interesting time, haven't we?" Jasper says.

"That's one way of putting it. I'm personally not comfortable going there, though. I've got some experience of this from managing my team, but that's as a manager with HR and Occupational Health guiding me. What on earth do we do when facing it one to one?"

"I think we have to trust our instincts, Simm."

"Go on then, Yoda."

"If we're feeling out of our depth, beyond our knowledge or competence, then I think we just call it."

"Meaning?"

"Meaning, we tell the coachee that we think the discussion is moving towards something that's beyond what we believe to be the contracted coaching boundaries. We help them seek alternative support, if that's what they want, but we make it clear it's not something that really falls within our agreed coaching domain or even our skillset."

"Well, well."

"Well, well, what?"

"You're not as stupid as that haircut makes you look, are you?"

"It's the new Yoda-coach look – all the fashion with us super-coaches. Anyway, I thought you said it looked OK?"

"I lied." Simone smiles and blows a kiss.

… *Click* …

SATURDAY, ELEVEN O'CLOCK, outside Hampstead's red-tiled Tube station.

"*Boo!*"

"You bugger, you made me jump."

Jasper hugs Simone and, stepping back, waves open his Crombie by way of introduction to his new neighbourhood. "Whaddya think?" He beams. "Far cry from Croydon, innit?"

Simone looks up and down the village high street. A post-apocalyptic vibe hangs in the air. Just a few pedestrians and motorists that seem to be moving slower than in pre-pandemic times, more relaxed, or curious, or cautious. She notes the peeling plane trees that line both sides of the street, adding to the village air. "You're not just a bugger, you're a lucky bugger. Look at this place. Is this really London?"

Jasper nods an imbecilic grin.

"How have I never been here before? It's only halfway up the Northern Line. I know I popped into your place on the way up to the Lakes, but I didn't see any of this." She faces Jasper. "You know I hate you, don't you?"

The gently ascending Victorian townhouses, the clock tower and the crimson telephone and post boxes, all give the elevated village a timeless feel. Jasper hooks his arm into Simone's, and they stroll off up the slumbering high street.

"So, what's the plan?" Simone asks.

"Well, I promised you the heath, didn't I? And Highgate Cemetery."

"Of course. How could I forget? More boneyards."

"And there's the Freud Museum, but that'll have to wait till lockdown's lifted."

Simone chuckles. "You still haven't had a girlfriend since Flo, have you, Jasper?"

"Nope."

"Strange that."

"Behave." Jasper squeezes her arm with his. "And

when it's all open again around here, there's plenty of shops and cafes and delis and more shops if that's madam's desire."

Well, it is a long time since madam set foot inside a shop Simone thinks as she eyes the hipster fashion of the few other pedestrians. She jabs Jasper with her elbow. "See the rainbow scarf that woman's wearing?" She discreetly nods towards a tall bohemian woman overtaking them on the otherwise deserted pavement. "Find me a shop with one of those and buy me some coffee and cake. Then I'm all yours ... and Marx's."

"Oh, you've been researching the old bones buried at Highgate, then?"

"Perhaps. But seriously, first coffee and cake."

They walk in silence as Simone takes it all in, admiring the independent shuttered shops and empty cobbled lanes running off to the side. *Lucky, lucky bugger.* They approach the top of the high street and Jasper nods towards an old iron bench next to a small window offering deli takeaway treats. They settle on the bench, and Simone crosses her legs

"Tartan Doc Martens? Funky."

Simone crinkles her brow. "Problem with that?"

"Well, this is Hampstead, darling."

"And I bet two miles in any direction is still a dump, so get over it."

"Just kidding, Simm," Jasper says. "Is lockdown killing your sense of humour by any chance?"

Simone breathes out a listless sigh. "Sorry, it is somewhat." She eyes the deli chalkboard for a few moments and then looks back at Jasper. Following his stare to the far side of the road, her eyes land on a clothes rail inside a hippy boutique displaying a collection of rag-tag woollen hats, sweaters and...

"Rainbow scarfs!" she shrieks. "Perfect. I'm coming back for that when lockdown's lifted."

After purchasing two croissants and lattes, they stroll onto the heath, heading east. After an hour's meandering, they come to Parliament Hill, named in the Civil War, and at one hundred metres, stands as London's highest point. All the city is visible from here, from the West End to the City to the Docklands. The once towering landmarks of Tower 42 and St Mary Axe, the Nat West Tower and Gherkin, are now all but swamped by the new heavyweights on the block: the Trellis, the Shard, the Scalpel and the Cheesegrater.

"Look at that bloody Walkie-Talkie building." Jasper points to the bulbous mass of 20 Fenchurch Street. "What a monstrosity, and directly opposite the Shard, too. They should never have got planning permission for that thing. What were they thinking?"

Simone is now used to Jasper's rants about piles of bricks. *He's off again.* "No dear, that's shocking, dear. Come on, dear." She leads him by the cuff down towards Highgate Village and their two famous gothic graveyards. Built to address the over-crowded burial problems, this product and symbol of Victorian London sits enclosed and untouched and still homes 170,000 souls. They stand for a moment outside the old chapel entrance.

He's done it to me again. First that old fort in Cumbria and now this place. "Okay, let's see what we have here then." Simone strides towards the black iron gates.

The Lebanon Circle of family vaults sit beneath the roots of a yawning Lebanon cedar tree. Twenty Portland Stone catacombs housing the great and the good of Victorian London. Beyond them a network of dirt paths track through the low green canopy of the west cemetery, beneath which sprawls a patchwork of ivy-covered tombs, gravestones and obelisks. Tree roots bulge from under tomb slabs, displacing iron railings as they make their torpid escape. Railings that now cease to mark grave borders just prop themselves against tomb foundations in a vague continuation of their role.

Early spring sun casts long shadows through the trees, along the paths and across shadowy ivy-clad tombstones leaning at drowsy angles. Some strangers prop each other up like drunks in the afterlife. Other congregations lose all sobriety and fall together, tombstone on cross, on obelisk, on gravestone. Neighbours now intimately acquainted, or re-acquainted. Other lichen-covered crosses and tombstones dissolve into the forest where close trees reach out to greet them. They curl out their branches, hugging them closer in a tightening, decades-long embrace until finally close enough to whisper – *you're mine now*. Some residents of God's grand acre rest alone and others in company, choosing eagles or angels. Sayers, the celebrated prize fighter, rests alongside his marble mastiff *Lion*, who led a crowd of some ten thousand up the hill to his master's funeral.

Simone and Jasper follow the dirt paths aimlessly and silently until they emerge from under a low-hanging fir tree to an open patch.

"Who's that over there?" Simone points across the clearing.

"Looks a bit incongruous, doesn't it?" Jasper says, as they veer off towards a squat black block adorned with a large MM crest. "Whaddya know, it's Malcolm McLaren."

"Malcolm Robert Andrew McLaren," Simone reads. "Who was he?"

"Godfather of English punk. Obnoxious character, as you'd imagine. Bit of a blot on the London landscape, and still is by the look of it."

They stand looking at the sculpted bronze death mask leering out from the brutish granite slab.

"Buffalo Gals," Jasper whispers. "What was that all about?"

"No idea."

"No, I think he lost the plot after the Sex Pistols. And now look ... punk really is dead."

And good luck to it. "Come on, I want to find Karl Marx." Simone turns and heads back towards the path.

Jasper lingers a while. "Here's another fun fact," he muses aloud. "Alexander Litvinenko is buried here too somewhere. In a lead coffin twelve feet deep, cos of the radiation." He looks up. "Simone. Simone?"

Jasper catches up with Simone as she approaches a curve of brick mausoleums. Yellowing neo-classic facades sitting cheek by jowl embedded into overhanging rhododendrons – like a skull's grin. Their stone facades crumble but their heavily mossed doors still keep the curious at bay.

The tendrils of an overhanging tree lace tightly around a small monument where Simone stops. "Some of these looks like Angkor Wat in Cambodia, don't they?" She tugs at a branch. "I've seen it in *National Geographic*. Do you know where I mean?"

"Certainly do," Jasper says. "Another destination on my ever-increasing list of places never ventured to."

"Of course. How is the gap year plan progressing?"

"Bit old for a gap year now. One might have to think of it more as a sabbatical."

"Well, whatever one decides to call it, is one any nearer making a plan?" Simone runs her fingers along the vice-like branches. "After your split from Flo in the Lakes, you certainly looked like a man wanting to wander."

"I did, but I've got this place up here now, so maybe in a year or two."

Simone nods over towards the skull teeth mausoleums. "You're not getting any younger, you know."

"I know." Jasper kicks the bottom of the grassy tomb. "Memento mori."

What? Simone snaps her head up. "Get you, with your Latin."

"Yeah. That's why I come here. Medieval monks had skulls on their desks, and I've got this place. Keeps your eye on the prize, doesn't it?"

"Which is?"

"No regrets. Nothing missed, nothing wasted," Jasper says.

Simone explores behind the leafy shrine, then sticks her head out from the side. "So, what's your view of it all?"

"Of?"

"Death."

"Well, there's a nice Saturday afternoon topic for you."

"Oh, come on. You brought me to this old boneyard, Jasper, so death can hardly be a taboo subject."

"True. You go first. What's your view?"

"No chance." *You're not getting me that easy.* "This rotting spot was your idea, so you go first. What do you think happens to us when we've shuffled loose of our mortal coil?"

Jasper walks across the path and sits on a stone bench outside the vaults. "I think it's all bobbins personally."

Simone joins him. "Bobbins?"

"Yep, that's my verdict."

"What, no eternal happy ever after? No heaven or hell? Is that what you mean by bobbins?" Simone idly digs two holes in the dust with the heels of her checked boots. *I love these boots. I don't care what that misery thinks.*

"Yeah. I've concluded that I'm definitely an existentialist at heart. I just can't subscribe to any religious or spiritual ideas. I'm not a raving atheist like that scientist bloke, what's his name…? Richard…"

"Dawkins?"

"That's it. He's amusing to watch on telly when he's debating with religious folk isn't he? He gets himself into a right lather."

"I know. I actually saw him at a book signing in Charing Cross Road once, and he was getting really worked up during the Q&A session with someone trying to spout their dogma at him. They should've known better than to try to convert Richard Dawkins, of all people."

"I'm not like that. I really am live-and-let-live when it comes to that stuff. Every single person has the right to believe whatever they want to believe. But I just can't fathom it. I see why people would want to believe in something after death – it's pretty scary to think of it being the end of it all. But that isn't enough for me to subscribe. I can see why we're superstitious as a species, to fend off that fear and anxiety, but at the same time, that awareness kills dead any chance of me having any of those beliefs myself."

Simone meditates on her air-cushioned soles, kicking into the dirt.

"Which is going to make my next coaching assignment very interesting."

"Really, why's that?" she asks.

"They assigned me someone who is renowned for her religious beliefs. Nice person, just very, very religious."

"Oh, wow, that is going to be interesting."

"I know. I bet it will play havoc with all the transference and counter-transference stuff. Anyway, that's me. What about you, what's your view?"

"Exactly the same as yours," Simone says.

"Fair enough, asked and answered." Jasper slaps his palms on his thighs and stands up. "Come on then. Let's find comrade Karl, then try and get some lunch."

Simone smooths down the two dirt piles with the toe of her boots and stands up.

"If the pubs were open, I'd suggest The Flask in the village." Jasper says. "I took Flo there a few years ago, and she copped for the most expensive Pimm's in North London. Being a Highland lass, she didn't like that. I don't think Mr Marx would approve either. *'Workers of the world unite. You have nothing to lose but your chains...'* And your twelve quid! Come on, let's go."

"ANOTHER DAY, ANOTHER Zoom eh, Simone?" *God help us.*

"Don't. It's driving me crazy."

"The novelty is running a bit thin now, isn't it?" Jasper drums his fingers on the side of his laptop screen. "Any idea when we're due back into the office?"

"I think there's an announcement on Friday with a proposed timescale. Maybe then we can have a go at some in-person coaching, which would be novel. How are your sessions going?"

"Yeah, wouldn't that be a treat?" Jasper says. "I think the coaching's going okayish so far. No out-and-out calamities." *So far anyway.* Jasper daydreams out of his window towards the ash and elm treetops in the distance. "I have noticed one thing, though."

"Go on."

"I'm really tuning into this transference thing. I know Freud was a bit bonkers and had a few crackpot ideas…"

"Yes, and yes," Simone says.

"And I know we've laid a lot of them to rest now, but some of the other stuff still seems quite useful."

"Like?"

"Well, his transference idea, for one. Since I read about it, I'm really aware of it when working with my new coachees."

"Really?"

"The conversations we have are pretty deep, right?"

Simone nods.

"I mean, not psychoanalysis deep but still pretty deep and personal for conversations between peers and colleagues."

Simone nods again.

"As soon as I meet a new coachee now, even though it's mostly through the screen at the moment, I feel myself having a reaction to them. It's weird, like first impressions on steroids. Even before they open their mouths, I'm reacting to them. I'm learning how to keep tuned in to these feelings and managing them before they start to manage me. In theory, great, in practice, not so easy."

"An example?" Simone asks.

"Sure. I've got one senior manager who I've really

been struggling with for a couple of months now."

"What's the problem?"

"Basically, he's a real entitled so-and-so."

Simone involuntarily splutters into her green tea. "You OK?"

"Fine. I see why you automatically laughed the other day when I told you about my own coaching faux pax. It's hysterical."

"It is?"

"Yeah. Not funny about the coaching work, just funny about what a dog's dinner we're both making of it, despite our training." Simone continues to chuckle. "Dear me, we've still some way to go, haven't we? So, tell me about this fellow, then."

"He's from the top-top floor and I really like him, but frankly, he's driving me nuts. I know technically it's not supposed to matter if you like your coachee or not, but I can't help wondering what difference it might make."

"Interesting thought. I'm not sure I've had enough sessions with enough people to get a sense of that yet. On the one hand, it shouldn't make any difference, as you say, but on the other…" Simone taps her teacup in time with the discussion she's having in her head. "If the key coaching conditions are things like warmth, empathy, positive regard, non-judgement etcetera, aren't these all things that will come easier if you naturally like a person?"

"I assume so," Jasper says. "But maybe that's where the training comes in. I think it's supposed to help you suspend your own personal view of things, to make sure you treat your client *tabula rasa*. Keeping all of your own views and biases out of the equation. Meeting them as complete equals, human to human, regardless of whether you'd go dancing with them at the weekend or not."

Simone smiles. "I can't quite imagine you dancing somehow."

"Well, you know, back in the day maybe. Anyway, I've been doing a bit of reading around each of the coaching modalities we've been learning, and both existentialism and gestalt quote a guy called Martin Buber who describes it as an *I-Thou* encounter. The human-to-human encounter, that is, not the dancing. In contrast to the more transactional way people usually interact with each other, which he describes as *I-It*."

"You've got to slow down on that reading, Jasper and let me catch up. I don't want you just throwing me out scraps like this."

"I don't want to over-egg the Hampstead thing, but it really helps to have a load of second-hand bookstores around. At least, when they're open."

"Yes, not too many of those in Ealing."

"Amazon stretches out that far, though, doesn't it?"

"You don't know the half of it. Mr Bezos and I have become very close these last few months. I'll reacquaint myself with his book department at the weekend. What's your first recommendation?"

Jasper doesn't skip a beat. "Irvin Yalom."

"Who?"

"Trust me."

"Okey doke, he's on the list. Which one?"

"Any, to be honest. Are you a fiction or non-fiction gal?"

"Fiction."

"Then I'd start with *When Nietzsche Wept*. Imagine Fredrich and Freud co-coaching each other and you've got the drift."

"Crikey. OK, it's on the list. Anyone else?"

"Manfred Kets de Vries."

"Mann Vrey Ket, what?"

"Hah – Kets de Vries. He's a business school professor who applies his traditional psychoanalysis training to contemporary leadership coaching, especially group coaching. Fascinating stuff, done in a completely non-psycho-babbly way."

"Okay. Book recommendations for him?"

"Literally any of them. They all combine theory, anecdotes, parables and metaphors. A really rich way to learn about what we're doing here."

"Wow, you're tearing ahead, Jasper. Who's doing your day job while you're reading all this?"

"Let's just say I'm using lockdown to master the dark art of delegation."

"Fair enough. So, tell me about this coachee from the top floor."

"Well, he's a humorous guy for starters, which, for me, helps."

"Whys that?"

"I find people with a sense of humour seem to possess greater perspective somehow. I'm not sure if it's chicken or egg or even if they're connected, but they seem to go together to me."

"Makes sense," Simone says.

"He also seems to be a decent guy. He seems decent with his team, reasonable with his colleagues and fair with his clients, a decent, all-round good bloke."

"Then you're going to have to enlighten me. Confidentiality accepted because he sounds like an ideal coachee to me."

"There's just one specific area I really struggle in my work with him."

Simone looks at Jasper expectantly.

"Don't laugh." *This is going to sound weird.*

She mimes a zip across her mouth.

"He keeps referring to his deal with the cosmos."

Simone's hand shoots up to her mouth.

"You promised, Simone Marshall."

"I'm so sorry." Simone hiccups. "The cosmos? And this is someone on the top floor?"

"Yep, but it's not what you think," Jasper says. "He's not spiritual as such. He just has an unholy sense of entitlement that he attaches to this one abstract thing – the cosmos."

"Go on."

"He believes that as he has put his time in at the firm, he absolutely, definitely, categorically, and without question, should be rewarded with exactly what he wants."

"Which is?"

"Directorship. No ifs, no buts. And he believes this so uncompromisingly that it keeps hijacking the rest of our work. He not only expects it, he demands it."

"OK."

"But do you hear that word, Simm?"

"Demands?"

"Yes, and the word behind it?"

"Expects?"

"*Should.* Remember our conversation back in the café about Ellis and his *shoulds*?

"I most certainly do." Simone blushes. "I also remember crying in front of you when you were asking me about my *shoulds*. Not my finest hour."

"That seems a long time ago now, doesn't it? Our first taste of coaching, and now look at us – we're doing it."

"After a fashion, and with varying degrees of success, it would seem," Simone says. "So, what happened to this guy?"

"He continued on, session after session. Demanding and unconditional. Oblivious to the rest of life's vagaries. When it comes to his career, he seems to lose the perspective and nuance that he normally displays. He becomes helpless."

"Helpless is a pretty strong word."

"I know, but I don't know how else to describe it. He won't work, he won't brainstorm, he won't problem-solve. It all just comes back to his *shoulds*, about what he's entitled to. He goes from intelligent problem-solver to unreasonable and entitled. It's bizarre." As Jasper stares down at the camera, something clicks into place. "But you know what I'm just flipping realising, talking this through with you?"

"Go on."

"I should just CBC him, shouldn't I?"

"Say again."

"I should do the cognitive coaching with him. Taking him through all his *shoulds* and getting him to dispute them in a structured rational fashion. What a numpty. Why didn't I think of this before?"

"We are still novices, Jasp."

"I know." Jasper lightly knocks the side of his skull with his near empty tin water bottle. "But it would be helpful to remember all this stuff at the time."

"Anyway, Mr Numpty, how does this all relate to transference?"

"Oh yes, I'd forgotten all about that." Jasper sips some water. "Well, I joust with him. He likes the rough and tumble of debate, so I get stuck right in with him. Instead of getting him to challenge his thinking in a constructive coaching manner, I just play devil's advocate. And probably not a very helpful one at that."

"Sounds quite tough for a novice coach to be fair." Simone says.

"I guess, but the point is, I'm letting his stuff trigger my stuff."

"In what way?"

"I should get him to explore his thinking objectively, but because I'm getting all heated about it, I don't. I joust with him in a way that stops us working in a more structured, positive fashion."

"Right." Simone says.

"And so, when he's whinging and moaning about all the injustices of this company-cosmos equation, I get frustrated, I poke at him and the coaching falters."

"Because?"

"Because I'm a muppet."

"A numpty *and* a muppet? That'll look good on your CV." Simone claps. "Seriously though, what's the stuff that's going on for you in all of this?"

All energy abandons Jasper, and he falls back into his chair. "You know my story, Simm." he says. "I'm stuck down in the engine room getting beaten over the head with daily tech and ops data, which I've done religiously and brilliantly for years, if I say so myself. And I've never seen so much as a hint of promotion or progression." His gaze returns to the distant treetops. *I don't know why I'm not job hunting myself, come to think of it. Maybe me and Simm could set up 'Yoda-coaches Inc'.*

"And? What's that got to do with your coachee?" Simone asks.

Jasper blinks. "Absolutely nothing, of course," he says. "That's the whole point. When I listen to this highly experienced guy, talking about how the universe is so unfair and he should be on the Board, I feel myself going off on this internal tirade about how he should be grateful for what he's got, blah blah."

Jasper gurns into the camera. "I know it's not him that's giving me the rats. It's me and my stuff. So, I just have to manage that, so it doesn't interfere with the coaching, don't I?"

"That's some Sigmund stuff in action right there," Simone says.

"It is. I need to coach him properly and not just push him around about taking more personal responsibility. That's clearly me talking to an issue that's more mine than his."

"Like me and my coachee, who wants to change jobs?"

"Exactly. If he wants to take control out of his hands and place it way out into the cosmos, then that's his choice, isn't it? I shouldn't be so involved or invested. It's not my life or career. I should roll with it and work with it, rather than simply react to it."

"So, what happened to him?" Simone says.

"In the end, it mired our coaching down, as I couldn't figure a way through it."

"And now?"

"He thanked me for our robust debates, signed off with HR, and went on his merry way. He's probably out there somewhere now, sparring with the cosmos."

Simone hugs her stomach and doubles up. "Oh my God, what a pair."

JASPER SCANS THE hotel lobby. *Guy reading the FT maybe? Bloke on his mobile? Chap loitering at Reception?*

"Mr Oran, is it?"

Jasper spins round to see his new coachee eagerly holding out his hand. "Hi. Luke? Nice to meet you."

With lockdown starting to lift, in-person coaching

is becoming possible, and it takes as long as their handshake for Jasper to conclude that he's probably going to like Luke. His beaming smile and chubby, warm face somehow signal that they will enjoy some good open discussions together.

"I hope you don't mind meeting here?" Luke says. "I'm doing some IT consulting for the airport, so it's very handy. It's a real pain to leave site completely at lunchtime. You just won't get a parking space when you come back on."

"No problem at all. Glad to be out of the house and off Zoom." Jasper waves to some seats in an empty corner. "Shall we grab those?"

"Great. I hope you don't mind us meeting somewhere so public."

"I'm OK with it if you are. It's only our introductory chat after all. Shall I get some coffee?"

"Oh, I'm sorry, I took the liberty of ordering already. I hope that's OK."

"Perfect." Jasper smiles, studying Luke a little more closely as they take their seats. *He seems a nice chap, but that's the third apologetic utterance in a row. I wonder if that's anything to do with why he wants coaching.* "So, Luke—" Jasper opens his notebook. "—the purpose of this initial conversation is just an exploratory chemistry meeting."

"Oh yes, yes." Luke nods keenly.

"And what that means is you and I discuss what it is you think you want to get from coaching."

"Oh yes, I see."

Jasper lets his last sentence hang in the air. He immediately warmed to Luke, but he already senses that he could be a very passive client. Pleasant and keen but submissive. That is, reliant on Jasper, or any other coach, to do the heavy lifting during their coaching sessions. It's too early for a loud alarm bell to be ringing, but there's a faint chime that puts Jasper on alert.

"The idea, Luke, is for you to tell me what brings you to coaching. What you think you might get from it and how you think I might help you with that. Then I'll tell you if it's something I think I can help you with and answer any questions you might have."

"OK, I see." Luke sits upright cradling his coffee cup in his lap. "I see," he repeats.

It is very early in his coaching career, but Jasper has already learnt one crucial lesson – don't take responsibility for your coachees' learning. You can help them and support them. But you cannot do their learning for them. Coaching is not a one-to-one lecture or training seminar. You don't teach your coachee anything directly, but you most definitely help them learn, focus, develop, and grow, sometimes in staggering and unanticipated ways.

Luke seems a little lost in the headlights, so Jasper decides more structure may help.

"Let's take it a step at a time, Luke. What made you request coaching from HR?"

"Well—" Luke places his coffee down. "—I've taken on this new IT project here at the airport and it's going to involve a lot of key stakeholder management. That's not something I've done before, so I thought it would be helpful to get some guidance on that side of things."

"What do you mean by guidance, Luke?"

"I'm not entirely sure. That's where I thought you might be able to help me."

Jasper's distant chime increases a few microbars. "OK, that brings us neatly to how you think I can help you. What exactly would you like to get from our conversations together?"

Luke shifts in his chair, flattening his wispy blond hair with a chubby hand.

Jasper sees his discomfort but is resolute in not rescuing him from it. He has learnt that this is an important part of the process and can achieve two things. First, it shows clearly that this is an active, not passive, process. Coachees cannot sit back and hope to learn directly from the coach – they learn through the process. And that process requires them to turn up, ready to work.

Luke taps his crossed knee, looking down intently at the coffee menu on the table.

The second point, Jasper reminds himself as he resists breaking the silence, is to let the coachee experience a few minutes of what that will be like. This is often awkward for the coaching client at first. They are used to having both their heads and the airwaves full of noise. Particularly in modern business organisations, where the static on the airwaves can be colossal.

Jasper sits quietly, watching Luke. He briefly thinks back to when he and Simone discussed the nature of silence whilst doing their training in the Lake District. They discussed how coaching can help quieten people's internal echo chamber just by giving them the time and space to think. Like fitting their echo chamber with acoustic cladding.

Aha! Speak of the devil. Jaspers eyes widen expectantly. *We appear to have some signals emerging from the quiet.*

Luke gives his knee a concluding tap and looks up. "Giving it more consideration than perhaps, I had up to now, I think it might fall into two distinct categories.

"Excellent, go on." Jasper notices Luke's cheery veneer has gone, and he now seems more serious and genuinely present.

"I think I need help with stakeholder management, but I think this breaks down into two further subcategories."

"OK."

"One part is the technical aspect of stakeholder mapping and analysis. But the other is the influencing element of it. And I think it's that I might need to discuss with you."

"OK. Say a little more about each of those, if you could please, Luke."

"Well, the stakeholder mapping and analysis is quite straightforward, really. I learnt all about it in my MBA and then, more recently, on a project management course. So, I've got all the various tools that I need for that, I think."

"Great, and the other aspect?"

"I think that's about how I behave with all these various people and groups. How I manage our interactions most effectively, that sort of thing."

"What sort of thing do you mean exactly, Luke?"

"Well, it's about me, I guess, isn't it?"

Jasper consciously sends Luke an affirming and encouraging smile. *That's more like it. Now we're getting to it.* "What sort of things around *you* do you think we need to explore, Luke?"

"I'm not entirely sure." Luke taps his thighs with both palms. "I've been told in the past that I come across maybe a little bit…"

Jasper nods encouragingly.

"Maybe a little bit…"

"Maybe a little bit…" Jasper repeats back.

Luke taps his thighs quicker and looks over each shoulder.

"Luke?"

"Weak."

"Oh," Jasper says. *Oh? What the hell was that?*

"Oh?" Luke repeats.

"Sorry, Luke, what I meant was that must have been very hard to share. Especially at our first meeting. How are you, sharing that with me?"

"Ambivalent." Luke pierces Jasper with suddenly flinty eyes.

Well, that rosy veneer evaporated pretty quick. "Do you want to delve straight into this, Luke? I don't mind, but I don't want you to feel you have to. It is just a chemistry session, after all. Have you met with all your other potential coaches yet?"

"I have, and I don't think either of the other two are appropriate matches for me, actually."

"Do you mind me asking in what way, Luke? Knowing that might help me if we're to work together."

"I think you might hit the sweet spot," Luke says, through a thin smile.

Jasper is suddenly unsure of his footing. In an instant, Luke has shifted before his eyes. Unnerved, Jasper draws on some basic training and repeats back what he considers the hot words in what his potential client has just said.

"Sweet spot?"

"Yes. I think the first coach would have been too easy on me. Too flouncy. Let me do what I like and congratulate me either way."

"OK." *Why do I not like the sound of this?* "And the other coach, Luke?"

"Well, he seemed a bit of a twat."

Twat! WTBF? Why is he saying that, and to me? "How so?"

"He seemed to know all of my answers before knowing any of my questions."

"Really?" *This dude has gone cold.*

"Yes. It was a half-hour chemistry conversation, and, in that time, he must have given me at least three pieces of advice."

"Really?" Jasper can only repeat.

"Yes, Jasper, really. And though I know little about this coaching, what I do know is that I don't want to be lectured to."

Okay, this is getting a bit freaky. What the hell happened to the happy chappy from the foyer? "No, quite right, Luke. Coaching should definitely not be a lecture."

Luke slowly shakes his head without saying a word or breaking his stare.

"So, I might be somewhere in between too much and not enough then?" Jasper half jokes.

"Something like that."

Okay, I think I've had enough now. "Well, Luke. I think we've got enough for this session. Now all we have to do is report back to HR and say whether we'd like to progress."

Luke stands up and holds out his hand, his warm smile returning. "I look forward to working with you, Jasper."

FOLLOWING HIS SESSION at the Heathrow Hilton, Jasper has arranged to call in on Simone and stay the night. He parks in a space behind the lost-looking shopping parade as per Simone's directions. He retrieves his overnight bag from the boot and gazes around. *What a dump. What's Simone doing in a place like this?* Jasper locks his briefcase in the boot and turns around to see a cloud of local youths gathering behind him. One of them mutters something about his Mercedes in a slang sounding vaguely Vulcan.

"No, bugger off, you can't look after my car. And if my wheels are gone when I get back, I'm nicking your bike to get home on." Jasper navigates his way through the boys, all far too old to be riding BMXs. He finds Charlton House and is buzzed through the main entrance into a surprisingly smart lobby with red-carpeted stairs up to Simone's first-floor flat.

"Nice gaff, Simm." He says, strolling into the living room.

"Numpty."

"Well, it is. What's wrong with it?"

"It's bland and dull and worst of all..." Before he can sit down, Simone waves him over to the glass doors and pushes him out onto the balcony. She points down to the sad, neglected pedestrian quadrant below. "It sits right above that."

Jasper scans and nods. "I've already had the pleasure of negotiating my parking arrangements with the resident youth. Did you have to run through that lot every night before lockdown?"

"Not when I was driving. There's an integral basement car park that brings me straight in thankfully."

"Well, it's conveniently situated for all the ... er ... amenities, as the estate agents might say."

"Certainly is." Simone retreats into the lounge. "I've lost count of the times I've woken at midnight wondering where I might get my next helping of crack kebab from."

Jasper settles on the settee. "Hello, Snowy." He leans down to stroke the cat moving through a figure-of-eight around his ankles. "Oh, I see now why you've called a brown cat Snowflake. That little white dot on its nose looks just like a…"

"Snowflake."

"I've not noticed that through the screen. She's usually showing me the other end of things. Aren't you Snowy? You charming little creature." He tugs her tail and glances up at Simone. "How long have you both been here now?"

"A few years. I thought it would be close to my folks and handy for the Tube and the motorway." Simone fumbles with a bottle and a corkscrew. "Which it is, but four years is quite enough now. I only rent, so I'm not even sure why I'm still here."

Jasper picks up the two chunky tumblers on the glass coffee table. "Very continental."

"I can't see me being here for much longer," Simone continues as she fills the tumblers. "Since our trip to the Lakes I feel really claustrophobic here. There's literally nowhere to walk to or get air. I'm not saying I need to live somewhere like there, but I definitely need more space than I've got here."

"I get it, Simm, really, I do. Let's have a proper look at that view." Jasper takes his glass over to the doors and walks out onto the small iron balcony. He leans over and watches the local youth comings and goings below. Much shoulder-knocking, hand shaking and fist-bumping. *Well, they all seem friendly enough.* Then he watches the same ritual over and over. *You wally, they're dealing.* He glances back inside to see Simone staring zombielike at the wall, cradling her tumbler. He gazes over at the distant lights of Heathrow. Five minutes pass before he walks back in. "Simm … I've got a weird proposition for you."

"Oh God. What is it? Please don't make it too

weird. I'm really not in the mood for *weird*."

Jasper moves in front of her gaze. "Move in with me."

Simone tilts her head and squints. "Look, Oran, I said if you came to visit, you could have the spare room. One drink in and that offer remains the same, so I think it's a tad inappropriate to be talking about cohabitation, don't you?"

"No, I'm not talking about cohabiting in that sense. I mean flatmates. You rent this place on your own, don't you ... lovely as it is. And I also rent a two-bed place. So that's four overpriced London bedrooms between us when we only need two."

Simone continues to squint, sipping her wine.

"And I'm not being funny, but you get a far better class of druggie in Hampstead, you know. Writers and artists all doing whatever they're doing in cosy privacy behind their sumptuous curtains. Not public like out there." Jasper nods towards the balcony and shakes his glass. "It looks like you can't even get to the off-licence without running the gauntlet."

Simone twists her finger around Snowflake's tail.

"You should probably think about saying something, Simm."

She holds out her glass for a refill. "Thanks."

"What, for the vino or the flat share?"

"Both."

"But it's a time-limited offer. There' are a lot of bohemian junkies out there just begging me for a Hampstead timeshare."

"I thought it was Highgate."

"It's all the same when you get up by the heath, you know. And I tell you, after Streatham and Dagenham and all the other places I've lived, it feels beautifully hobbit-like up there. With the hills and the heath, it's like a hobbity dingily dell crowning smoggy old London." Jasper fills Simone's tumbler. "There's even open-air classical concerts in the summer."

"Oh, fuck off." Simone takes a gulp of Burgundy.

Jasper shrugs. "'Tis true."

"COME LOOK AT your room," Jasper excitedly leads Simone up a narrow stairway to the second floor, straight through her new bedroom to the balcony doors. "This view is yours."

Simone briefly looks, then yanks Jasper into a hug.

"Is madam satisfied with her new accommodation arrangements then?" Jasper muffles into Simone's new kaleidoscope scarf.

"I can't tell you." She pulls away and steps out into the view. "Look!"

"I know, I live here." Jasper laughs. "It's all there. The Telecom Tower, Saint Pauls, the Shard. And there's enough room in here for your desk and PC. So, when you're done with all your Zooming for the day, you can sup your green tea and contemplate life while looking out over dear old London Town."

"I really appreciate this, you know."

"I know," Jasper says.

"But you also know this is a platonic arrangement, don't you?"

"Don't flatter yourself, Miss Marshall. That dreamy view comes at a price. I need nine hundreds of your hobbity-dollars on the first of every month to keep the dream alive – *comprende*?"

"Totally—" Simone says, swinging round. "—and my first domestic contribution is to get some Sunday groceries. Gimme half an hour and I'll be back with lunch."

"No arguments here." Jasper waves her past.

Two hours later, Simone lurches back breathlessly through the front door and into the kitchen. She dumps the grocery bags onto the breakfast bar.

"You OK?" Jasper asks.

Simone grins. "I've just done one brief food shop and at least four people conversed with me. Four."

"Yeah, sorry about that. For Londoners, they're quite social up here."

"That's not the point."

Jasper starts to unpack some loose-leaf green veg, and unfamiliar fruit. "What's the point, then?" he asks.

"I didn't get a single lewd or aggressive comment, Jasper. Or anyone trying to sell me drugs. No drugs, no abuse, nothing – just kumquats." She beams. "Bloody kumquats!"

"I think we got you out of that place just in time, Simm." Jasper holds out a small luminous fruit. "Bloody kumquat?"

Chapter Four
COACHING, LIFE AND LEADERSHIP

JASPER AND SIMONE are heading to Gloucester to another training retreat with their pre-pandemic coaching tutors, Alan and Alison.

"It'll be good to see the Als again," Simone says.

"Yep. I wonder what authentic leadership group-coaching even entails," Jasper says.

"No idea. It's good to get three days out of the office though, whatever's involved." Simone taps the top of her steering wheel. "Assuming she makes it. My poor ailing Volvo."

Jasper coughs.

"I know it's not well–" Simone says, as it misses another engine beat "–but I'm not taking it to a Dignitas dealer. I love this car and until Facilities come up with something as endearing, I'm sticking with her."

"Her?" Jasper whispers into his McCafé.

"Of course – Her."

"Right."

"She's seen me alright on many a mile has Val. We're road-sisters."

Jasper looks over. "Val?"

"Volvo Val. What else could I call her?" Simone says.

"Nope," Jasper says, sliding down in his seat. "That's perfect." He taps the dash. "Nice to meet you,

Val, even if it is on your way out."

Simone slaps Jasper's arm. "Shh. She'll hear you."

"Not over that misfiring she won't."

They travel slowly west through Oxfordshire under the vast sky that drifts over the Cotswolds plateau.

"Would you just look at that sky," Simone says to herself.

Eventually, reaching the far western edge where the plateau drops down to Gloucestershire and the view spills out into the Severn Valley. Jasper points to a sign for Alford poking out from an overgrown hedgerow. Simone steers the Volvo down a single-track lane threading through a tunnel of wych elm and whitebeam until they emerge back into the sunlight and opposite the yellow stone village planted on the opposite side of the valley – picture-perfect. Alford's church spires and stone slate roofs sit timeless among fields of blazing rape and spring barley.

"Wow. That's it over there." Jasper points to the baronial Alford Manor standing to the edge of the village.

Simone nurses Val through the manor's crumbling entrance pillars onto the yellow stone-chip driveway. They get their first proper sight of the house, melting perfectly into the landscape, part Cotswolds Stone and part ancient wisteria vine. Simone brings the ailing Val to rest alongside a limestone wall lined with human-sized hollyhocks fluttering in the breeze. Once again, they crunch their trolley bags along a gravel driveway up to a large slab of wooden door to meet the Als.

"Miss Marshall and Mr Oran." Alan beams. "As I live and breathe." For a second time, he welcomes his students through a huge oak door frame. "Come in. Come in, sit." He clears the cushion ballast from a low settee in the entrance lobby and stands back, folding his arms as they sit down. "So, how have my favourite students been?"

"Oh, please, Dr Wainwright." Simone says. "I'm sure you say that to all your students."

"Yes, I do, to be fair." He takes their coats, smiling broadly. "But I only mean it half the time."

"This feels very familiar Al," Simone says, looking around, "but dare I ask what you have in store for us this week?"

"Well, what did I say last time you asked me that in the Lakes?"

"Hmm ... something like 'Lots of good stuff and you won't be the same when you leave.'"

"And were you?" he asks.

"Actually–" Simone looks back intently at Alan, "– no, I wasn't."

"Then guess what?" he says.

Simone puts a finger on her chin. "Ditto?"

"Ditto indeed." Alan smiles. "How about you, Jasper? How's life been the last couple of years?"

"Oh, you know." Jasper reclines to gaze up at the heavily beamed and cobwebbed ceiling. "Same as with many folks, I guess. Lockdown was weird, novel and boring, in equal measure."

"And did you get to use your coach training?"

"We did. Our company assigned each of us a few coachees to work with online, wanting to get a return on their investment as quick as possible, I imagine."

Alan places a tray of coffee onto a huge wooden strongbox in front of the settee. "So, how did you find coaching virtually?"

Jasper glances over at Simone, who rolls her eyes.

"Weird, novel and boring in equal measure again."

"Go on." Alan slides their cups along the top of the ancient wooden box.

"On balance, I'd say it worked OK. But because we were new to it, our learning curve was steep. I think I speak for us both when I say we made plenty of rookie errors along the way."

"It's not a science, guys. You'll always have key choice-points in your coaching – shall I go this way or that – and you won't always get it right. In fact, there probably is no such thing as a right way. Just judgement calls that turn out more, or less, helpful for the client. That's why I prefer longer coaching assignments. It takes time to get to know a client, what they'll respond to and how to work with them."

"I can hear you lecturing them already, Alan, and the poor souls have only just got through the door."

"Alison!" Simone jumps up to hug Alison who's emerging through the kitchen doorway.

"Alan's right though. I had one client, near to here actually, who I worked with for a year. It was business, business, business. He kept reporting to me like I was a shareholder or something. Context is key, sure, but I'm there to learn about him, not his latest business conquests. Nice to see you, Jasper." Alison walks past and squeezes Jasper's shoulder and then perches on the creaky wood box to pour a cup of hot water.

"You too. I can't believe it's been two years already. So, what happened?"

"Eventually, he learnt how to use me and our time together more effectively. He was very task-focussed, which is nothing unusual at that level, but also incredibly unreflective and incurious. So, for quite a long time, he tried to control our meetings in much the same way I imagine he controlled many of his other work meetings."

"That's fascinating," Simone says. "What did you do?"

"Gave him time and space, initially, to establish our trust and rapport. Remember those core conditions?" Alison says with a teasing smile. "Then gradually I turned the conversation more and more towards his own inner experience, rather than dissect minutely the gains and losses of the various conflict scenarios he seemed supremely skilled at generating. Gradually, I was able to move him towards an examination of the part he played in all the conflict swirling around him." She plops a slice of lemon into her water and takes a sip. "Point is, and I can see why, in hindsight, there was no way he would have trusted and opened up to me in just a few short sessions. He was one mightily defended individual, and we needed time to navigate that. Quite a bit of time, it turned out." Alison carefully puts her water down onto a coaster.

"And the outcome?" Jasper asks.

Alison stares into her cup. "It was a very happy-ever-after outcome … eventually." She looks up. "As Alan says, along the way there were many, many choice points. And in the early stages, with someone like that, there was a lot of trial and error. But you learn to manage it in such a way that it helps build the relationship rather than damage it."

"How?" Jasper and Simone ask in unison.

"All in good time." Alan stands and picks up both coats. "Come on, you guys, it's Sunday. Take a few hours off, enjoy the gardens and the sun, and we'll see you first thing."

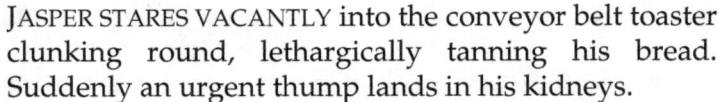

JASPER STARES VACANTLY into the conveyor belt toaster clunking round, lethargically tanning his bread. Suddenly an urgent thump lands in his kidneys.

"Mother of God!" Simone rasps into his ear.

"Jeezus, Simone. Ow!"

"Oh, don't be such a wuss. Have you seen this agenda?"

"Yeah, I was reading it through last night. Why?"

Simone recoils, momentarily speechless. "And that's it? You were *just* reading it through?"

"Yeah, looks interesting." Jasper rubs his kidneys with one hand and picks up his tanned toast with the other. "What's the big deal?" He moves down the breakfast line.

"Oh, I don't know. Maybe just three little words." Simone sticks to his heels.

"Which are?"

"Past, present, future," she says into his other ear.

"Yeah, what's up with that?"

She pulls Jasper's sleeve and attention away from the cereals. "Bloody past, present and future, Jasper."

"Uh-huh."

"We've got to stand up in front of the group and talk to them about our past, present and future. Are you not listening?"

Jaspers looks over Simone's shoulder at the juice bar. "And?"

"And?" Simone looks at Jasper, wide-eyed. "OMG, Jasper. When all around are losing their heads…" She picks an apple out of a wire basket and taps it on his forehead. "And you're not, then you're clearly not paying attention."

Jasper darts around her and scoops up a box of

muesli and a grape juice then walks briskly towards an empty bench. An agitated Simone follows. "Do you know anyone else in the group?" she asks.

"No, of course not. Why?"

"So, you're happy to talk about yourself in front of a bunch of strangers, like you're just chatting with your mates?"

"Probably prefer it, to be honest." Jasper holds out his hand. "Kumquat?"

"Funny." Simone slides down onto the opposite bench. "I think I'm on the verge of a panic attack here, Jasper, and I'm not kidding."

Jasper stirs his tea. "It won't be that bad."

"No…?" Simone's tapping feet turn into leg and body shakes. "No!?"

"Bloody hell, Simm, I thought you were messing." Jasper jumps up, rushes around the table and shoves alongside Simone on the bench. He puts his hand on her back as she gulps air, quietly telling her to just breathe, slowly, breathe, slowly, breathe…

"I'm going to be sick." Simone jumps up and heads to the canteen exit.

After twenty minutes, Simone emerges from the Ladies and joins the back of the small group as they file into the drawing room. Large furniture has been pushed to the side against the high bookshelves and a circle of green upholstered chairs sit ominously in the middle of the room. The group gradually populates the circle, and an odd silence descends. The Als just sit and watch and smile until everyone has taken their seat.

"Good morning, everyone. I'm Alan and this is Alison and we'll be working with you over the next three days. We've had the pleasure of working with everyone here at different points, but currently you're all strangers to each other in the group, bar a couple of exceptions."

Simone scans the group to identify the other *exceptions*.

"However, I guarantee you'll all know each other well enough by the end of our time together."

Anticipation sparks the air and while everyone's eyes are darting about, Simone stares straight at the ceiling, tapping a fingernail against the chair's tubular frame. *Just breathe ... it'll be fine. Good training and good experience. Just breathe...*

"I'm not saying that you'll remain on each other's Christmas card lists forever–" Alan continues "–but you will certainly become pretty important to each other over these next few days. And maybe beyond ... who knows?"

Individuals shift in their seats, and the apprehension continues to ripple around the room.

"As you all know, the subject of this coaching group is authentic leadership. A topic very live within leadership at the moment." Alison continues. "And to help explore your own authentic leadership we'll be exploring your lives. Tomorrow we'll be looking at your present and on Wednesday, your future. But today we begin by looking at each of your pasts." She looks slowly around the group."

Jasper watches Simone sitting on her hands and winks at her from the opposite side of the circle.

Simone narrows her eyes. *Don't wink at me, Oran.*

"As you'll have seen on the agenda," Alan continues, "we'll be asking each of you to take a turn in the hot seat where you'll share your thoughts on our three key topics: your past, your present and your future."

Simone winces.

"The idea is that your authentic leadership comes

from a full understanding of your values, character and purpose. All of which are rooted firmly in your own personal autobiography. Hence the need to explore your past, present..."

...and future. Yes, we get it. Simone's toes start tapping along with her fingertips.

"We won't be directly teaching you anything during these sessions other than about leadership temperament on day two. We simply help you explore and understand these autobiographies."

Simply? Simone continues to tap.

"To that end," Alison picks up, "we ask all of you to support each other's exploration through coaching. That is, when a person is in the hot seat, you listen to their story and then ask them questions, give feedback, offer observations, etcetera."

Sounds delightful. Simone scans the bookshelves. *What I wouldn't give to be curled up back in my room with one of those.*

"We ask," Alan goes on, "that you offer no advice to any group member at any point, because that's not the point, is it?" His eyes seek confirmation of understanding and some nods surface around the circle. "You all get plenty of that at work, but not here. Here is a place to think. So, you can help each other's thinking by asking quality questions and by offering insightful feedback and astute observations. Advice and suggestions will only close down that exploratory thinking." He stays quiet to ensure the message finds its mark. "You've all been on our coach training, so I'm hoping you get what we're asking and why we're asking it. Yes?"

"Yes," several people answer.

"Great. The first task is a nice introvert one where we ask you to draw your lifeline on a piece of flip-chart paper marking out your highs and lows, your major challenges, successes, life lessons learnt, and the values you have developed as a result of all of this." He walks around the circle and starts handing out flip-chart paper and pens. "Start where you wish and include only what you think is important. Make sense?"

A few hesitant nods. "OK. Find a space." He claps his hands. "We'll reconvene in thirty minutes."

Frozen to her seat, Simone looks at Jasper. He offers a sympathetic crooked smile and a shrug and then walks to the back of the room with his paper and marker pen.

Tra la la, tra la la la … one banana, two banana, three banana, four, Simone hums. *OK, Marshall, you've got this.* Simone slowly walks her own paper over to a large oak desk under a stone leaded window, jabbing the pen into her hip as she goes. *Tra la la, tra la la la…*

Hunched scribbling continues for half an hour as the Als walk silently around the room watching the charts, graphs, paths and squiggles all take shape. Everyone scribbles, then ponders, then scribbles some more.

"OK, guys, time's up. Back in the circle, please." Alison takes her seat and waits patiently for everyone to return. "So?" She smiles. "Who's up first?"

"I am," Simone blurts out. *Sod it – let's get this over with, otherwise I might just bolt.* She strides up to the flipchart with her pre-prepared sheet and secures the page with tape. *OK.* She turns to the group of seven faces looking up at her expectantly. The group of Jasper, two Als and four strangers. Four strangers who she's just about to tell her life story to. David – the law firm partner, pleasant, posh but scary. Dawn – the NHS director, brilliant, ballsy and scary too.

Suzanne – the research fellow, striking, ethereal and scary. And Hugo – the HR director, intense, scary and chewing a Bic biro.

I'm sure you're all lovely people, even if a little scary, so here goes. "Hi, my name's Simone and I'm from Ealing, born and bred." She points the marker pen to the top of her page, marked out as a graph. "And my story starts here."

The ethereal Suzanne follows Simone, then the pen-chewing Hugo and then they adjourn for lunch. Jasper shifts from one foot to the next outside the restaurant and Simone emerges again from the Ladies, approaching, head down and rummaging through her purse.

"How are you doing, Simm? You OK?" Jasper lightly touches her elbow. Simone looks up, beaming.

"What?" Jasper gapes.

"That was amazing."

"What?" Jasper says again. "I mean ... what?"

"Amazing," Simone repeats. "You wait till your turn, you'll see." Simone breezes into the restaurant and grabs a tray. "Don't just stand there." She looks back at Jasper rooted in the doorway. "It's pretty intense, so you'll need your carbs. This moussaka smells fab."

Jasper lifts his jaw and joins Simone at the buffet. He follows her around, studying her silently as she spoons selections from the salad bar. They find an elegantly laid table in a bay window overlooking the lawn.

Jasper puts his plate of moussaka down. "You're gonna have to help me out here, Simm," he says, as Simone crunches on a carrot. "At breakfast you were freaking out and by lunchtime you've gone all Buddha-like. I couldn't believe you went up first.

What's occurring?"

"I went up first because it was a case of then or never. But as soon as I started talking through my lifeline, a whole different feeling came over me."

"I saw and I couldn't fathom the change. You looked so calm and centred." Jasper taps Simone's knuckles with his fork. "Like them out there, look." He points his fork through the window at some peacocks gracefully pacing the lawn. "So, what happened?"

"Too early to say for sure." Simone watches a peacock approach their window to peer in. *Beautiful.* "It was a game of two halves, as you blokes keep saying about football." Jasper raises his eyebrows. "First, there was the experience of talking through my entire life story. Which, if you'll forgive the potty mouth, I thought I would crap myself about." Jasper nods. "But it was a revelation. I couldn't believe the themes and connections I saw just by talking it all through to the group. Things that I've been oblivious to my whole life suddenly emerged clear as day."

"Really?" Jasper asks.

"Totally. Just reflecting on your personal highs and lows and the lessons and values that develop as a result – amazing."

"And then the Q&A?" Jasper asks. "How was that?"

"Brilliant. It was so powerful seeing your own life story up there. What you choose to draw in the first place and then how you decide to understand it, articulate it and share it with the group. And then, to be quizzed on it and asked about the various connections and influences and how this might have affected this, that or the other. I saw themes and patterns in my life that I'd simply never noticed before. Literally, in one half-hour session, it answered more questions than I can tell you."

Jasper sits back and folds his arms.

"I felt vulnerable in front of the group, sure, but with the conditions Al and Al create, I also felt safe and supported. Their no-advice ban works wonders. It means nobody's telling you what you could or should have done. It's all geared towards insight and understanding. And under those conditions that exercise…" Simone stops herself. 'Actually no, it wasn't an exercise – it was an experience. And under those safe and contained conditions, the experience was nothing short of a revelation." Simone taps the window with a fingernail to attract the majestic visitor from the lawn. "A giddy revelation." She looks over at Jasper, who has said nothing for a while. "You OK, Jasper? You're looking jaundiced."

"What the hell do I tell them about my family, Simm?"

"Oh, shit. I'd completely forgotten about that. Shit, shit, shit. Sorry, Jasper, I was so absorbed in my own hissy fit I totally forgot about the implications of doing a lifeline for you. What are you going to do?"

"I really don't know." Jasper checks his watch. "But I've got about twenty minutes to decide."

Thirty minutes later Jasper is standing in front of the flip chart. "Hi, all." He scans the group and fiddles with the marker pen between his fingers. "I'm from various parts of London, also born and bred, and I've chosen to start my lifeline here." He points his pen to the start of a meandering pathway. "It's the year my mother and I discovered we were just one of two families my father was simultaneously raising."

Hugo's biro drops into his lap.

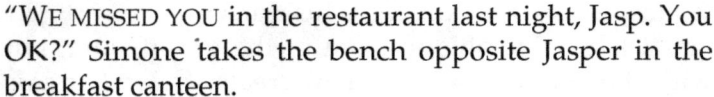

"WE MISSED YOU in the restaurant last night, Jasp. You OK?" Simone takes the bench opposite Jasper in the breakfast canteen.

"Yeah. That lifeline exercise left me with a bit of a hangover to process, so I just got room service."

"You OK though?"

"I think so. As you said, that whole public disclosure experience is pretty powerful. Who'd have thought that talking to a group of strangers would be so…?"

"Intense?"

"Definitely that. But also, somehow, normalising."

Simone smiles.

"And clarifying. Hugely clarifying. You throw your stuff out there and the group somehow acts like a hall of mirrors. But rather than distorting what you say, it helps you see it more clearly." Jasper gulps his last mouthful of coffee. "Ready for round two?"

They cross the parquet floored hallway back into the drawing room.

"Good morning, folks. You all survived day one I'm pleased to see and have come back for day two, which is encouraging." The Als exchange a brief glance.

What does that look say? Simone looks around the group. *That they knew we'd be back? Or they're surprised we are?*

"Yesterday, we looked at your lifelines and what values emerged as a result. We heard about such values and principles as teamwork, competence, support, contribution, collaboration, wisdom, vision, independence, self-respect, self-awareness, challenge, growth and, of course, honesty, integrity and authenticity. We heard about the importance of understanding your own version of each of these and, importantly, being aware of where they originated from." Alan looks over to Alison.

"And today we look at your leadership character and intelligence by examining what's called your leadership temperament," Alison picks up.

"What if you don't have any leadership character or intelligence?" Dawn quips.

The group laughs, and the Als just smile.

"It's a fair question," Alan says, as the mirth subsides. "But you all have leadership character and intelligence. So, the only real question is, what is it and how do you use it?" The group listens in silence. "Think of your temperament as your leadership orientation – what you focus on and prioritise." Alan walks across the room and turns the projector on. A collage of leader images appears on a piece of bare wall between the bookcases. "Forgive the mini lecture, as there's a lot of info to impart in this section. But I promise it's the most I'll talk for the whole three days, so bear with me." Alan leans on a high-backed chair next to the projector table. "Although social factors such as family, education and economics play a significant part in character development, the temperament you're born with is probably a more fundamental determinant of your behaviour than all these factors combined. This leadership temperament is an extension of your personal temperament and that comes from your biological inheritance. Ultimately, this creates a natural predisposition towards patterns of behaviour that will appear consistently throughout your life."

The group remains quiet. Then after a minute, David asks, in a lawyerly way, "Example?"

Alan nods but doesn't rush to answer, allowing David to pick up on the resonance of his own style of contribution.

"OK," Alan says in time. "Politics aside, what would you say are the fundamental differences between Boris Johnson and Theresa May?"

Laughter breaks out again through the group.

"May is thoughtful," Dawn says, above the noise.

"Too hesitant," Jasper says.

"But Boris is bold," says David.

"Too reckless," Simone says.

"Beneath that boldness he also seems strategic in his thinking," Hugo says. "Which we need."

"But May is down to earth and cautious," Suzanne says. "Which we also need."

Alan lets the energy run through the group. "What about Jacinda Ardern?" he asks.

"Hell of a human," Suzanne says.

"Bleeding-heart Liberal," David says.

"Jeff Bezos?" Alan presses on.

"Future emperor of the world," Dawn says.

A socio-political debate continues, which the Als let run for exactly two minutes.

"And that is precisely the point." Alison's volume brings everyone back to attention. "You can debate their success and effectiveness, but in the end, you'll likely all still agree on one thing, their leadership character. That is, their leadership temperament."

The circle settles.

"And when you tune into it, you'll see it everywhere – with the people you lead and coach and work with every day," Alan says.

Furtive glances cross the circle.

"For example, you have strategic leaders like Elon Musk or Bill Gates," Alan says. "Disrupters and innovators. Leaders who think in big-picture, long-term, abstract ways, who can conceive of innovations long before the rest of us even realise the current stuff isn't up to snuff. They think of the yet un-thought of." Alan stands back from the chair. "Again, forgive the didactic piece. Strategic leaders are born problem-solvers and think in terms of possibilities and probabilities and ignore traditional views and ideas."

Alan leans under the projector table and grabs a snooker cue. "I took the liberty of borrowing this from the billiards room last night." He taps the end of the cue onto the images of Bill Gates and Elon Musk.

"These leaders are ever on the lookout for problems to solve. If they don't have a problem to solve, they set themselves one just to exercise their minds. They are natural reasoners and greatly value intelligence. They despise any form of stupidity, especially in themselves. They have great systems intelligence and want to understand and master everything that is important to them. Can anyone think of any other examples?"

"Abe Lincoln?" David says.

"Brilliant example." Alan taps the tip of the cue on the projector table. "Read the book of his life – *Team of Rivals*. It's a master class in systems thinking and strategic leadership. Any others?"

"How about Karl Marx?" Simone says.

"Another brilliant example. Marx was an outstanding theory builder. His most popular one, after communism, of course, was called historical materialism. He created an entire theory that argued history was the unfortunate result of materialism rather than ideas. What a brain. And I think he's actually buried here somewhere in England."

Simone can't help herself and raises her hand. "I

can actually see the cemetery where he's buried from my bedroom in London."

"Seriously?" Suzanne says.

"Yes, all thanks to my new landlord here, Mr Oran."

"Well, that's definitely what we all want to hear about over lunch. But in the interim, let me finish this lecture then I can sit down." Alan taps his cue on the wall. "Above everything else these strategic leaders must be competent. Their very self-esteem depends on it. For them incompetence is abhorrent. However well they have done in the past, that's only a benchmark for determining future performance and success. They must achieve again and again and always at a higher level. This hunger for greater achievement pushes them throughout their entire lives and careers."

The circle of gathered professionals gives a collective nod.

"Then you have the tactical leaders who are bombs of energy that come alive in times of crisis or emergency. They love a messy merger where they can swoop down onto burning platforms and play the corporate Red Adair."

Several foreheads in the circle crinkle.

"Really? Red Adair? No?" Alan looks around the group.

"Oh yes," David says. "American chap who came over to tackle some North Sea oil-rig fire we had back in the eighties."

"That's him," Alan says. "These leaders are maestros of performance under pressure. And this guy came over at the back end of a career fighting oil-field fires in Texas, Asia and South America. His biography *Red Adair: An American Hero* is quite the wild ride." Alan reveals a pre-prepared flip-chart page reading

Mini-lecture warning!

"These leaders come alive in the immediate, concrete and frantic here and now. But they're maybe not so great at thinking and planning for an imagined long-term future. And if Mr Adair is a bit before your time, think of Trump. Putting all morals and ethics aside, he's a leader rooted in the ever-present. Creating issues and causing troubles that he can negotiate and battle all day long. Not perhaps the leader you want working on the nation's long-term global plans, but maybe one you might want on your side, slugging it out on the rough and tumble of the campaign trail."

Alan points the tip of his cue at the images of JFK, Ronald Reagan and Vladimir Putin.

"Their attentiveness to the immediate environment and drive to optimise their position within it is unequalled. Whether skirmishes and manoeuvres on the sports field or in the boardroom, tactical leaders are always scanning for opportunities, always looking for the best angle of approach that gives them the greatest advantage and chance of success. They notice the smallest detail in their surroundings, which allows them to exploit whatever resources are at hand to their advantage. With their ear to the ground and their finger on the pulse, they can always spot an opening or an opportunity." Alan exaggerates a deep intake of breath.

"Nearly there," Alison says.

"Tactical leaders are most at home in a concrete world. They have little interest or patience for mere abstractions that they believe are of little practical use. They see themselves, and want to be seen, as bold and competitive. Their self-confidence, self-respect and self-esteem depend on their ability to act daringly, impressively and competitively. They will not be outdone or overtaken and always have one eye on the next plot or the next shot."

Alan taps his snooker cue on the face of Winston Churchill. "Has anyone read the exploits of Mr Churchill in the Boer War? If something does not excite these leaders, they'll look for something to be excited by. They detest routine and the status quo and need action. Vigilance and opportunism make them great negotiators who can spot things that give them an edge where others can't, so they make excellent trouble-shooters. Business often uses the analogy of the burning platform when the heat is on and talk of metaphorical fires that need fighting. Well, when it comes to manoeuvring through these intense management crises, the tactical leader with their incomparable nerve and skill is the unmatched Red Adair of the business and political world."

Again, heads nod around the circle.

"Then you have diplomatic leaders," Alan continues. "Leaders gifted at working the connections and relations between people while also grasping and understanding what's in each of their interests." He reaches for his water bottle. "Think of the typical U.N. Secretary General, such as Kofi Annan, Ban Ki-moon, and Antonio Guterres. They could give us all a masterclass in diplomatic leadership. Listen to their speeches and you'll hear them peppered with grand ideals for human health, justice and prosperity." He puts down his bottle and holds up his palms. "Grand ideals perhaps, but isn't that what you'd want from the world's most senior politicians? We don't want them bean-counting, picking fights or conducting time-and-motion studies, do we? We want them to lift the world up to be a better place, no?"

Alan taps the *mini-lecture* flip-chart page again with his snooker cue. "Diplomatic leaders deal with people in a skilled, tactful and sensitive manner. They have an instinct for seeking the common ground and can interpret everyone's communication positively. They have a gift for putting themselves in another's place and so are well-equipped for the task of influencing people's actions and attitudes. As leaders, they inspire their people to grow and look to forge unity among them. Individuals drawn to diplomatic leadership are often deeply disturbed by division and discrimination and so the most famous idealist diplomatic leaders are those who forge change in human rights using themselves as their principal instrument of leadership. Think Nelson Mandela, Mohandas Gandhi and Martin Luther King."

Alan leans on his cue. "Any other examples you can think of?"

"Che Guevara?" Hugo offers.

"Possibly."

"Barack Obama?" Suzanne adds.

"Probably."

Alan stabs his snooker cue onto the projected face of Henry Ford. "Finally, we get back into the concrete in the form of the logistical leaders. Think Henry Ford and other captains of industry. Leaders who are masters of organisational structure and efficiency. Supply-chain specialists who can eke out every cost saving and efficiency to be had. They gain advantage, not by disrupting the status quo, but by streamlining it."

Alan draws a smiley face on the flip chart and scribbles, *Last lecture, I promise!*

"Logistical leadership is about the efficient and effective procurement and distribution of material goods that are vital to the success of any institution. Such leaders are enormously creative in seeing that the right personnel have the right supplies in the right place at the right time to get the job done. They care about being reliable, particularly in the maintenance and continuity of their organisations. Logistical leaders know that change is inevitable and often necessary, however, they find it unsettling and so may resist it if it comes at the expense of time-tested ways that have served the institution well so far. The most talented logistical leaders often become managers, executives and leading business figures."

Uncle Fester's doppelganger totters through the door with the coffee trolley.

"The logistical leader respects law, order, authority, tradition and caution. They have a deep and abiding sense of responsibility to any group they belong to. Whatever the group is, they strive to preserve and protect it, which means duty, obligation and loyalty, which they take very seriously. Nor would they have it any other way."

Alan again points his snooker cue at George Bush Senior, Gordon Brown and Margaret Thatcher. "Others?" He turns to the group.

"Colin Powell?" Dawn asks.

"Yep."

"George Washington?" Hugo says.

"Hundred per cent. These individuals predominantly orientate their leadership towards the preservation of the organisation's rules, traditions and protocols. George Washington was exactly the man for the job in establishing and, more importantly, stabilising the U.S. republic at that time in history. By all accounts, he wanted to retire back to his family farm after his first term, but seeing the precarious nature of the fledgling republic, he agreed to stay on a second term to help ensure it was properly established and stable."

Alan rests his snooker cue against an ornate iron radiator. "These leaders are renowned for enormous effort and determination along with impressive moral stature and unswerving loyalty." He returns to his seat. "So, in a simple militaristic summary, the tactical leader wins the immediate intense firefight. The logistical leader wins the battles by establishing invincible supply lines. Strategic generals in the war room plan how to win the overall war. And the diplomatic leaders work out how to secure the lasting peace once the war is done."

"So, that's them," Alison says, "but we're here to talk about you. Which type of those leaders do you think you are?" She scans the group. "David?"

David brings his gaze down from the ceiling. "Well, as you describe it, I'm almost certainly tactical. It was the idea of the sport that brought me to Law. Even after thirty years, I still get a thrill from the politics, the games, and the power plays. All of which I still excel at, if I say so myself."

All eyes are on David.

"Especially when we're battling other barristers in court. I love the pressure and performance of it all. I have out-of-body moments when I'm looking down from the ceiling fan and watching myself in the star role of a *Crown Court* episode. That's a reference for the older generation in the room."

The group stares in silence.

"I hate the detailed paperwork of my job, but I love the tough client negotiations and most of all the blood sport of the live trial. I live for those days."

"That sounds a pretty high-octane existence, David," Alison says.

"It is. And now I'm approaching retirement, I'm not sure what I'm going to replace that with." David clasps his hands on his lap and returns his gaze to the ceiling.

"Thank you, David. How about you, Dawn?"

"As you describe it, I think I'm big-time abstract," Dawn says. "Everything to me is a puzzle or a problem. I'm not so bothered about the people side of things, which is maybe a bit of an odd thing to say as an NHS director. But I just love the intellectual challenge of working out systemic organisational problems. 'Design then redesign' could be my motto – just for the hell of it. The NHS is possibly the best place for me in that respect."

The group nods in unison.

"Hugo?" Alan says.

"HR for me is all about structure and stability, so it's the logistical leader for me. I see HR's role as making sure everyone is in the right job and that they then have the right tools and resources to do that job to the best of their ability. All for the good of the organisation."

David clamps his hand to his chin to stifle a yawn.

"I know it may not be the high drama of the courtroom, David, but someone has to run the companies your clients come from."

"Forgive me, Hugo. Continue."

"It's the building blocks of any effective organisation and a role I take with the absolute seriousness it deserves. It can have its own moments of high drama too, I assure you." Hugo glances sideways at David.

"Thank you, Hugo. Suzanne?" Alan says.

"Research to me is the answer to all life's problems," Suzanne says faintly. "So, I guess it's the diplomatic and idealistic leader for me." She looks around the group. "There is, of course, the never-ending gamesmanship of grant applications and research publications." She stares into the middle of the circle. "But at its core, and my core, I know it's still a noble cause. And it is a cause. It's not a job or even a career. Medical research for me is a cause and a calling and I couldn't not do it."

The grandfather clock beside the coffee trolley chimes ten.

"Thank you, one and all, for that." Alison reaches down to a pile of A4 envelopes below her chair. She passes them to Alan, who circles the group, handing out one to each.

"This is your leadership temperament report we produced before the programme. We ask that you find a quiet space to read these through. Think about what resonance or significance it may have for you. When we come back into the group, we'll go around and hear from each of you in turn. About what you recognise in the report, what you agree with and what you don't, what seems important to you, whether it's new data, something you recognise or something just coming into focus."

She stands in the middle of the circle. "OK, folks, off you go, thirty minutes."

Everyone stands and mills about awkwardly for a moment.

"Hi, Jasper. I wanted to say that I thought your lifeline yesterday was really moving."

"Sorry?" Jasper glances up at Suzanne and then looks around to find Simone.

"I thought the way you described your family's history and how you'd still kept your senses was quite inspiring," she says. "Perhaps I'll see you in the bar later."

"Er ... yeah, perhaps." *Where are you, Simm?*

"OK, GUYS." AL waits for the chatter to subside. "The three chairs at the front represent three different perspectives on your leadership challenge – Self, Other and Situation."

The group look in silence at the chairs arranged into a mini horseshoe.

"Today is about the future," Alison continues. "So, we will ask each of you to talk about your leadership scenario from each of these three perspectives."

Jasper sits down next to Simone in the circle. "What are you going to talk about?" he whispers out of the corner of his mouth.

"It's got to be my potential career change, hasn't it?" Simone whispers back. "You?"

"Same – same. I've had enough. Time to take my frustrated talents elsewhere, I think."

"So," Alison announces, "Take five minutes, grab a coffee, then we'll start. Jasper, you're first up."

Simone pulls Jasper away from the group mustering around the hot water urn. "You've not said you were thinking of jumping ship," she says.

"Apt turn of phrase, Simm. You know I've been getting restless down in the engine room, and these couple of days have just brought me the crystal clarity I need." Simone nods him on. "I've run my course at our place. I think I want to try my hand at proper leadership somewhere, not just the pseudo-leadership-management thing I currently do."

"Any idea of what or where?" Simone asks.

"Absolutely none." Jasper beams.

"Me neither," she says. "I just don't want the route the firm has lined up for me. More tedious business meetings, which I hate, and less managing my team, which I love."

"You've not progressed your thinking about that, then?" Jasper asks.

"No. I'll take my thoughts into this SOS exercise and see where I am at the end." Simone nods towards the rest of the group, who are returning to their seats. "I'll catch you at lunch."

"Jasper, you're up." Alison waves towards the three empty seats.

"Okey dokey." Jasper stands up slowly. Simone taps his foot with hers and he heads towards the empty chairs.

"The first chair is Self," Alison says. "So, first, we'd like to hear about your leadership challenge from your own personal perspective. What are your thoughts and feelings about it, your concerns, hopes and fears, etcetera?"

Okay. Jasper nods.

"Then we'll move you to the next chair – Other. Here, we'd like to hear about this scenario from the perspective of other key stakeholders involved. Your team, your clients, your boss ... whoever you think is most central in this situation and upmost in your mind."

"Got it."

"Then finally we'll move on to the Situation chair where we'd like to hear from a detached, objective, factual perspective, as best you can."

"Got it," Jasper repeats as he takes the first seat.

The group stares hushed and expectant, and Jasper stares back. "Well, from the Self seat," he says, "I'm lost."

A stillness holds the group.

"Lost?" Alison says back.

"Seems so."

"Tell us more, Jasper."

"I've worked in my company for years. I don't mind it and I've not minded it for years. But for exactly the same number of years, I think I've fucking hated it."

Jasper clenches his jaw.

"I didn't know why I hated it until this week. Until I understood why it just doesn't fit with my personal and leadership temperament. The role needs tactical and logistical leadership, and I am so far out strategic. I just didn't know why I was so out of sorts with the role for so long."

"Can I ask a question?" David asks.

"Of course," Jasper says.

"How did you not realise you were in the wrong job?"

Jasper laughs. "David, I'm sure there won't be enough money in it for you, but if the Law Society ever strikes you off, you might think of a job in career counselling."

David smirks up at the ceiling.

"I don't know, David. I think, like a lot of folks, I had some disquiet about my place in life and work. But I couldn't figure out why. Didn't know if it was my boss, or my company, or what." Jasper looks over at the Als. "Seems it was my flipping leadership temperament."

Simone stares steadfastly at Jasper.

"My role wants me tactical and logistical and concrete, but I'm fundamentally abstract and strategic," Jasper continues. "For years I've been collating the data, and no-one has ever asked me what more we could do with it. How it could develop the company's direction or strategy. It's always just been a case of streamlining: faster and cheaper. Not, it would seem, what my brain is wired for." Jasper leans back in the Self chair.

"Thank you, Jasper. Now, would you mind moving over into the Other chair and tell us who that is?" Alison gestures towards the middle chair.

"I know this is going to be a tad abstract – surprise, surprise – but I guess the Other is actually going to be my career." Jasper gives the group an apologetic smile.

"Jasper, this is about authentic leadership," Alan says. "So, it's about your life, your leadership and your autobiography, and if that is at a crossroads that you're having to confront, then I'd say it's the perfect other."

"Thanks."

"So, what does your career have to say, Jasper?"

"It says…" Jasper screws up one side of his face. "It says…" He looks at the laden bookshelves and his attention drifts. An image comes into focus. He sees the library in his childhood home and a blurred image of his mother in a long hippie halter dress, a floating Renaissance vision waving him towards the bookshelves. *Come, Jasper. When you're old enough, we can read all these together. I'll even introduce you to your namesake, Karl Jaspers…*

"Jasper. Jasper?"

"Sorry, Alison. I disappeared somewhere."

"So, what does your career say?"

"I think it says–" Jasper nods emphatically "–I'm very fucking disappointed in you."

The sun glints in Jasper's damp eyes.

"Good work, Jasper," Alison says. "And what else?"

"It says it needs me to move on to somewhere where I can think bigger thoughts. To a world beyond SLAs and KPIs. But where?" He pauses. "Shall I nip into the Situation chair?"

"Sure, if you're ready."

"Well, this perspective is a bit more straightforward." Jasper says, rubbing his fingers across his eyes. "It's just about data: money, time, opportunity, prospects."

"Sounds like much more than data, Jasper," Alison says.

"You're right. Each of those could do with a good SOS-ing of their own, couldn't they?" Jasper laughs.

Alison looks back expressionless. "Maybe."

Jasper sits upright and puts his hands under his thighs. "The bottom line is…" He stares through the window and back to his childhood reading room. *'I'll introduce you to all these brilliant thinkers, my dear boy, and it will open your world–a world that will be yours–as long as you continue to question and listen.'*

"Jasper?"

"Sorry." Jasper wipes his eyes again. "Bottom line is … all of that stuff is on mortgage, isn't it?" He nods. "I'll probably leave it there for the minute."

"Thanks, Jasper." Alison looks out into the group. "That's the SOS intro done – now over to the group for questions."

"Well, I have one," Dawn says. "What on earth does 'on-mortgage' mean?"

"As it sounds," Jasper says. "Borrowed, loaned, in hock, not yours." He looks at Dawn. "Surely you can relate to that, working for our country's largest employer. One that will take as much of you as you're willing to give, regardless of its work-life balance policies."

"Humph," Dawn grunts.

"You'll work there, Dawn, till your time is done. You'll no doubt make a dink in things while they're on your watch, then you'll fall over, and they'll replace you. That's just how it is. You'll never be as important to them as they are to you. That's cycle-of-life stuff."

Dawn watches Jasper and says nothing.

"Again, can I ask a question?" David says.

"Again, of course you can, David." Jasper smiles.

"Now you've realised you are in the wrong job, what will you do about it?"

"David, David, David. If only I knew."

"You look like you might have something to say, Suzanne," Alan joins in.

"I do, thank you." Suzanne clasps her hands together and points the two index fingers to her chin, as if in prayer. "In the other chair, Jasper, you said your career is disappointed in you. So, what do you say back to it?"

Alison and Alan lock gazes.

"There's a question, Suzanne," Jasper says.

"Uh-huh."

He closes his eyes and glides back again. To a sunbathed room of musty books and oiled wooden bookshelves and a small hand holding out one of many books of questions.

"Sod it!" Jasper's eyes shoot open. "I say sod it, Suzanne."

Simone gives Jasper a sidelong glance.

"I've all of a sudden woken up. I've just realised that my career has been based wholly and solely on providing answers."

"And," David says.

"And, David, my old fruit, I don't think I give a rat's ass about answers – I think I want to follow the questions!" Jasper looks around at the vacant expressions. "Please tell me I'm not the only person in the room like this."

"I don't think you are," Suzanne says.

"Me neither," says Dawn.

"Thanks guys."

Silence settles on the group while they sit, processing.

"I think there's still a lot to be said for answers," David says.

"Absolutely," Hugo adds.

"That's as maybe," Alan says, "But here is not the place for them. Do you think Jasper himself got any insights from that last session?"

"Of course," Dawn says.

"Certainly seems so," David adds.

"And somehow all with no answers being proffered." Alan winks at Jasper. "The power of the question, aye, Jasper?"

SIMONE RESTS HER elbows on the dry-stone wall by the front lawn and gazes out across the elevated Cotswolds plateau. Cauliflower clouds stack in the still sky, and jasmine hangs in the air. She rips tufts of moss off the wall and drops them into the neighbouring field. *Questions, questions. Where to go? What to do?* She watches swathes of sunlight pass like torchlight over the landscape, illuminating one field, then another. *Questions, questions.* She drops another handful of moss as she hears a persistent crunch approaching.

"What are you doing out here, Simm?" Jasper leans on the wall alongside her.

"Just getting some space to figure out what I take into the session."

"I thought it was going to be about your job and career."

"It is. But it feels like there's something more to be understood. Something about my desire for change in the first place." Simone turns to look at the peacocks nutting about the lawn.

"Go on."

"That's just it. I don't know where to. I don't know why I'm not happy in my job. They give me more and more responsibility and opportunity. More pay and promotion, and I don't know why it's not enough. More than that, I don't know why I won't leave."

Jasper turns and stares up at the house's grand octagonal chimneys. "Maybe the group will help you figure it out."

"Maybe." Simone claps the moss from her hands. "Let's find out, shall we?"

They cross the lawn and head back inside. The rest of the group are seated in the circle and waiting for the Als to take their place.

"Okay, Simone. I think you're up." Alan smiles and nods towards the horseshoe.

Simone stands and heads for the horseshoe, humming, *One banana, two banana, three banana, four...*

"How are you feeling, Simone?" Alan asks.

"Um ... a little petrified," she says, and takes the Self seat.

"Well, we're all friends here now, aren't we?" Alan says. "So, tell us about your situation from the Self perspective."

Simone shrugs, apologetically. "To be honest, my situation is almost identical to Jasper's. I've been plodding along for several years doing perfectly well at my job, but now I've realised it's not what I want to do any more. I've got various leadership challenges I could explore, but they all feel insignificant compared to my main issue, which is that I think I want to move on, but I feel stuck. So, I guess my main leadership challenge is how and where I find my next leadership challenge."

The group is hushed and attentive.

Simone shifts in her seat. "It's taken me ages to come to this realisation, and now I have, I can't seem to act on it." She looks around at the faces in the group. "But I just don't know why." She turns to Alan. "I think that is what I want from this session."

"You ready to move to Other?"

"Sure." Simone looks down the room and moves towards the adjacent chair but stops mid-flow. She stands stationary for a few moments, glances back down the room and then sits down gradually with her hand over her mouth. "I think it has just come to me in this very second that the Other in this scenario isn't my boss or anyone like that … it's my father. My dear old dad – oh my God!"

David raises his eyebrows. Suzanne frowns. Dawn purses her lips and Hugo just blinks.

Simone looks straight through them all. "He's the one I've always mentally answered to about my career. The one I've had sitting on my shoulder the whole time." Simone's stare anchors onto a framed picture on the far wall. "The one I seek counsel from on all major career choices and decisions."

Simone backs slowly onto the situation seat without looking. "And that's what, or who, has guided me all my life. My father, the…"

Jasper turns around to see the picture Simone is glaring unblinkingly at – an original line drawing of the manor house plans.

"My father … the architect."

The group sit soundlessly waiting for Simone to continue.

Alison leans forward. "Thank you, Simone. What questions or comments are there from the group?"

"Uh-um." Hugo clears his throat. "Isn't that completely natural, though?"

Simone shifts her gaze from the sketch to Hugo with no change of focus or expression.

"What I mean is, aren't we always in conversation and competition with our parents? Forever trying to please them or outgrow them or do better than them?"

"I guess." Simone returns to the Self chair. "But what I've never realised until now is that he's, in fact, held me back."

Jasper now leans forward.

"I love him dearly, of course I do. I respect him intellectually and admire him professionally. Except, it would seem..." Simone puts her hand on her throat "...in one particular area."

David's interest shows through his imperious manner. Suzanne's frown straightens. Dawn's lips soften and Hugo stares wide-eyed.

"For all the wise counsel he's always given me, he's also hijacked me."

David's eyes narrow. "How so?"

Forgive me, Dad. Simone presses her palms to her cheeks. "Because he never took a risk in his life." She looks back up at the manor house blueprints. "I don't blame him. I understand, I do. His career was in a different era. But I've carried with me all this time his internal script about care and caution, always being careful. I don't think I've done a single bold thing in my life." Simone stands up, crosses the circle and walks between Jasper and Hugo up to the framed plans between the bookcases. *But that's him. It's not me. It was his time, not mine.* After a moment's reverie Simone sees in the glass reflection everyone turned in their seats to watch her. Feeling suddenly self-conscious, she twirls around and flips her palms up. "Ah, Jeez, but whaddya gonna do? I blame the parents."

The group erupts and Simone returns to her seat relieved at having turned her intense personal moment into one of comical effect for the group. *I don't think the Als will appreciate that diversionary tactic, though.* Simone glances over sheepishly as she passes them.

"What I'm beginning to realise," she continues when back in her seat, "thinking this through with the group, is it's clear that my poor dad's cautionary nature has influenced nearly all of my personal and professional decisions – or rather, indecisions. It's made me chronically cautious and indecisive. What should just be a sensible approach to life has somehow turned into a debilitating indecisiveness that's caused me problems my whole life."

"Example?" David asks, less lawyerly and more inquisitively.

"Well, until very recently, I lived in a rented flat in a crappy area of London, for no particular reason other than it was where I lived. For how long, Jasper?"

Jasper looks up abruptly from the carpet. "Er, four years?"

"Four years," Simone repeats to David. "And I've no good reason why."

"I see." David nods.

"How long have I been at my job, Jasper?"

Jasper smiles. "You're in the hot seat, Simm, but I think it's about twelve years."

"Exactly right." Simone stares at David. "And for no real reason there either, other than it's where I work."

"So, why don't you just move?" Dawn says.

"Exactly," Simone spits out. "Why don't I?" Simone slumps in her chair and wipes her mouth with the back of her hand. She glances again at the building sketch and catches Jasper's eye. She looks back at the two Als and nods towards the picture. "Because I'm scared. Obviously."

Hugo clasps his chin. Dawn scratches her head. Suzanne overbites her lip and David nods imperceptibly.

"Scared?" Alison gently repeats. "Of what?"

Simone grins and sits up. She looks at David, then Dawn, then Suzanne and Hugo. She looks across at the picture on the wall and then across to Alan and Alison. "Exactly." She shrugs. "Of what!?" She then turns to the group and her look lands firmly on Jasper. "Of what?"

FOR CRYING OUT *loud, every flaming time we get onto a motorway.* Jasper kicks Val's back tyre. "I think she's had it."

"I felt it coming a junction ago," Simone shouts down from the grass verge. "Not the worst thing that could happen."

"Nope, definitely not the worst," Jasper shouts back, hauling the emergency triangle out of the boot. "Not the best either." Jasper scrambles up the grass bank and flumps down next to Simone. They lie in the sun listening to the trucks thunder below.

"So," Simone says. "What would be best and worst?"

"What do you mean? The best and worst in this scenario?" Jasper looks over puzzled. "Or the best and worst of the big scenarios we were discussing in Alford?"

"Whichever," Simone says, shading her eyes with her forearm.

"Well, the best here is that we get collected by the recovery truck quickly and get home."

"Or?" Simone says from under her arm.

"Or the worst is that we crawl back round the M25 and along the North Circular. And then crawl back into our old lives, ready to crawl back into work first thing in the morning."

They hear a metallic clang below them.

"Hang on a sec, the triangle's blown over." Jasper slides down the bank, wedges a rock on one of the triangle's feet and then scrambles back up to see Simone snap her Galaxy shut.

"Who was that?" he asks.

"Liam from work."

"And?"

Simone leans up on her elbows and squints through the sunlight to the carriageways below. She ponders the traffic for a moment and then turns her narrowed eyes to Jasper.

"I just handed in my notice."

"No way!"

She smiles. "Yep way."

Jasper scrutinises Simone in silence for a few seconds. He then gazes up to watch the bellies of the long-haul flights slowly disappearing to God knows where. He closes his eyes and lets the sun warm his face. Then he smiles and without looking down extends his hand out to Simone.

"Pass the phone."

Contact us for training, development and support in all things coaching, inc:

Coaching / Coach Training / Coaching Qualifications / Coaching Supervision

3D Leadership Consultancy
www.3DLeadership.co.uk
info@3DLeadership.co.uk
+44 (0)7956 188645

Sign up to our mailing list to receive alerts about future publications:
www.3dleadership.co.uk/coachinglifeseries

www.ingramcontent.com/pod-product-compliance
Lightning Source LLC
Chambersburg PA
CBHW020256030426
42336CB00010B/785